Overheard from

"Professor Binder cares about his students and... think and ask yourself: How can I apply this to my reality and bring about justice?" ***Zyna A.***

"Perry provides a means of learning which applies to everyone in the classroom. There's a difference between being in class and wanting to be in class. Every lecture I attended, I can honestly say I wanted to be there." ***Stephanie B.***

"I will never forget coming back from surgery and the first thing Perry does is start the class on a welcome back chant for me." ***Kevin C.***

"Perry Binder is a rare nexus of a professor who does not merely teach; he inspires. He implores students to expand their horizons, think on a bigger scale, and pushes them to dream bigger and to confront challenges." ***Hannah C.***

"Perry's class was more than just another class for me, it was a decision-making catalyst, and had a huge impact on my future. His classes were the ones that I felt passionate about and never bored." ***Kevin Cr.***

"Binder is the Michael Jordan of teaching!" ***Harlem D.***

"Perry is so entertaining in the classroom that one often wonders why he hasn't taken up comedy as another career." ***Jennifer F.***

"I appreciated Perry's commitment to helping my classmates and me go beyond our limited backgrounds and cultures and blossom into informed and caring professionals." ***Anthony G.***

"Two essential lessons that Perry's class taught me are: important information is everywhere if we spend the time to look closer; and it's more meaningful to find humor in our daily lives than to live with fear, pessimism, or divisiveness. Those lessons go a long way toward finding happiness and reaching the success that we all imagine." ***Thomas H.***

"Professor Binder's class kept us engaged the entire time. The best part was that he actually motivated his students, making us WANT to learn and succeed." ***Anita K.***

"Professor Binder brought the classroom to life. In his class, I felt inspired and motivated to produce a level of work that met the passion he taught with. He made learning law enjoyable, relatable, and exciting, so much so that I decided to go to law school." ***Mhakai K.***

"I took every class that Perry offered and he was my most memorable professor. His classes were always full and the students were always engaged!" ***Wesley M.***

"Perry Binder was not only a Professor, but a Mentor. His classes were not about memorizing material, but taking it and applying it to real-life scenarios." ***Lizette O.***

"Perry Binder is a one-of-a-kind professor who makes complex legal studies entertaining, engaging, and easy to apply to real life. Of all my past business school professors, he's the only one whose classes and teachings I remember more than 10 years later." ***Andy P.***

"To have shared a classroom with Perry was not only a learning experience but a trajectory for life." ***Vincent S.***

"I wish I would have just gone to Perry Binder University! Perry's enthusiasm was contagious and my cheeks would be sore from laughing after every class!" ***Kevin W.***

Faculty endorsements for the author's last book, *Classroom LIGHTBULBS for College Professors*, are in Appendix M.

INNOVATIVE COLLEGE TEACHING

Tips & Insights from
14 Master Teachers

PERRY BINDER

INNOVATIVE COLLEGE TEACHING: Tips & Insights from 14 Master Teachers
© 2024 Perry Binder, LLC
All rights reserved

ISBN: 979-8-870510-51-4

No part of this publication may be reproduced or transmitted in any form, without the written prior permission of the author.

Excerpts from:
Classroom LIGHTBULBS for College Professors
© 2023 Perry Binder, LLC

99 Motivators for College Success
© 2012 Perry Binder, LLC

Unlocking Your Rubber Room
© 2009 Perry Binder, LLC

Interior Graphics
© 2023–2024 Perry Binder, LLC

Master Teachers retain the copyright to their contribution to this book and grant permission for its use in the book and the author's workshop materials.

Unless otherwise noted, all of the events in this book are true as the author remembers them. Names of individuals which appear in quotation marks have been changed.

Dedication

*To Barry Hantman
and in memory of Greg Stewart,
two Master Teachers.*

*To the many Master Teachers
I've learned from and continue to learn from.*

Contents

Preface ix
Introduction xi

PART I: Innovative Teaching Techniques

1. Teaching Philosophy and the First Day of Class 3
2. The Structure of Each In-Person and
   Online Class 13
3. Using AI to Enhance Classroom Activities and
   Student Projects 21
4. Preparing Students for Multiple Choice and
   Essay Exams 31
5. Teach to Your Strengths 37
6. Help Students Stay Engaged Through Exaggeration
   and Humor 41
7. How I Got Here 47

PART II: Innovative Master Teachers

8. Diana S. Barber, J.D. 53
9. Jordan (Jody) Blanke, M.S., J.D. 59
10. Yelena Abalmazova Chan, Esq. 63
11. Evaristo Fernando Doria, Ed.D., M.i.M. 67
12. L. Gregory (Greg) Henley, MBA, Ph.D. 71
13. Leila Lawlor, J.D., M.B.A., M.S., M.A. 75
14. Laura E. Meyers, Ph.D. 81
15. Isabelle N. Monlouis, MBA, DBA 87
16. Benita Harris Moore, Ph.D. 93
17. Carol Springer Sargent, CPA, Ph.D. 97

18. John P. Thielman, Esq. 103
19. Paul Ulrich, M.S., Ph.D. 107
20. Marta Szabo White, Ph.D. 113
21. Key Takeaway from Each Master Teacher 117

Epilogue 121
APPENDIX 123

    A. First Day of Class Story: Youthful "Offenders"

    B. Spelling/Grammatical Errors in Student Papers

    C. Sample Term Sheet

    D. Sample Module for Interactive Classroom Discussions

    E. Using AI to Develop Classroom Modules

    F. AI-Generated Demand Letter Assignment

    G. Project Based on Demand Letter

    H. Incorporating AI: Minor Tweak to Assignment

    I. Short Team Project

    J. Team Project Peer Evaluation Form

    K. Sample Essay Exam Question and Model Answer

    L. Calculating Course Grades for Graduating Seniors

    M. Faculty Praise for the Author's Last Book

    N. Classroom LIGHTBULBS Acronym

    O. Author's Publications

Acknowledgments 161
About the Author 163

PREFACE

"The master has failed more times than the beginner has even tried."
—Stephen McCranie, writer/illustrator

The goals of this book are to:

- share innovative, practical teaching tips I developed over time to keep myself motivated and students engaged; and
- highlight what inspires select colleagues to teach with creativity and passion.

Like many of you, I continually try new approaches to remain current and fresh. *Innovative College Teaching* contains my tried-and-true methods as well as a window into the process of tweaking and perfecting student projects and activities at different stages of development.

For example, last year I had a vague understanding of artificial intelligence or "AI." By Spring 2023, professors were concerned about the use of ChatGPT and potential cheating opportunities at universities. That summer, I decided to adapt and search for teachable moments. In Fall 2023, I created projects that required students to use AI. Time will tell how much refining I need to get the assignments just right.

Innovative College Teaching will get you to consider outside the-box ideas for your class, such as leveraging new technology in any discipline. For added measure, I invited a bunch of Master Teachers to join in the fun by offering their novel teaching techniques and insights.

Perry Binder
October 2023

INTRODUCTION

Embrace AI-generated student projects? Flip your online AND in-person classes? Administer open-note in-person exams? I know, but please keep an open mind.

Innovative College Teaching contains easy-to-replicate teaching tips along with key insights and inspiration from interviews with several Master Teachers. The book is intended for new or seasoned professors, lecturers, instructors, professors of practice, and part-time (adjunct) professors, as well as curious high school teachers. You will learn what makes the best teachers tick and read ideas on taking your skills to the next level.

Most of the books on college teaching are loaded with advice that *tells* you how to teach (Be passionate; Be flexible; Be yourself!), rather than *show* you by example how to teach. In Part I of this book, "Innovative Teaching Techniques," I will show you my teaching methods:

- how I conduct the first day of class;
- the icebreaker technique I use to start every class;
- how my online class closely mirrors my in-person class;
- why I rarely use PowerPoint;
- interactive classroom modules;
- individual and team projects;
- how to prepare students for multiple choice and essay exams; and
- an exam gift for graduating seniors.

Further, I provide examples of each teaching activity in a robust Appendix. For example, you can read:

- my project on how students are required to use AI to "write" professional demand letters to a company;
- a model AI-generated letter; and
- each prompt I used to create that document.

In the past, this task would take students a few hours to complete from scratch. Now, they get to do so instantly. They experience how AI can benefit their personal or professional lives and then reflect on the project's value through targeted questions.

In Part II, "Innovative Master Teachers," each professor that I interviewed responded to the following questions:

1. What inspired you to teach?
2. What teaching methods are most helpful in guiding students toward their goals?
3. What would you like to improve about your teaching?
4. What skills should be emphasized in high school to succeed in your college class?
5. What is the one thing you wished you would have known when you started your teaching career?/Do you have any last bits of wisdom?

I interviewed accomplished colleagues including a star adjunct professor for readers who teach part-time. They bring diverse teaching styles from varied disciplines, including Education, Entrepreneurship, Law, Science, Technical Education, and several Business departments. These individuals are not just knowledgeable. The words I use to describe them are curious and innovative. Their passion for teaching is contagious. Students gravitate to them. You will read stories about how a professor:

- gets students to co-design classes;
- develops cross-border interdisciplinary learning experiences;
- connects with non-science majors in a science course;
- uses intelligent agents that automatically send email messages to students if they miss a quiz or assignment;
- conducts "legal show and tell" to weave current news into course content and encourage class participation;
- inspires students to care about the written word because of her mother's inspiring childhood gift; and
- cultivates student curiosity while having them acknowledge that it requires vulnerability which in turn requires courage.

Throughout the book, I capitalize the term "Master Teachers" as a sign of respect for their years of service to the higher education profession. *Innovative College Teaching* was fun to write mainly because of their participation.

PART I

INNOVATIVE TEACHING TECHNIQUES

CHAPTER 1

Teaching Philosophy and the First Day of Class

Before I get into the mechanics of my class, here are my thoughts on the teaching profession:

Teaching Philosophy

Teaching is my professional passion. I believe that an effective teacher has the following qualities: empathy, enthusiasm, flexibility, and a desire to learn from colleagues and students. In class, I want students to be intellectually curious, work hard, have fun, and understand that there are no boundaries to their professional dreams. I try to accomplish these goals by giving them "real world" critical thinking exercises on business dilemmas.

I have great respect for how hard many of our students work in part-time or full-time jobs while trying to get a college degree. I am reachable seven days a week for them. While I cannot offer legal advice, I guide students to resources on handling their personal or professional legal issues, and help figure out when they need to hire an attorney. I also assure them that they can contact me in an emergency. In one instance, I walked with a student into a Rape Crisis Center. In another, I drove to a jail at 10:00 p.m. to speak with an incarcerated student. I have stayed in touch with some students for many years, watching them succeed in the business world and come back to my class as guest speakers.

I mainly teach law and ethics classes in the university's business school. Using actual cases, my students engage in frank discussions on what business activities are legal or illegal, as well as on what their "gut" says is ethical or unethical behavior. In addition, especially at the MBA level, I ask students to assess their levels of comfort when encountering legal risk in business. For example, students debate the value of enforcing employee non-compete agreements, and attempt to figure out the point at which keeping employees happy and productive outweighs some measures of "lawyering up" their businesses. It is easy for risk averse businesspeople to hire an attorney to write one-sided employment contracts. However, they should balance the leverage they have over employees to sign such contracts, with the effect that the contracts may have on worker morale and productivity.

For out-of-class activities, I believe that the internet provides the most significant innovation in teaching. It allows me to supplement textbooks with lively, current material, as well as supply practice-oriented information relevant to businesses in my state. In recent years, I integrated social media sites into my classes and have students search for and analyze appropriate and inappropriate postings, and how the comments would be viewed by a supervisor in a workplace setting.

I encourage students to be confident in their fact-based opinions and to continually challenge or "teach the teacher." For example, in my Internet Law class, students know more than me about emerging technologies such as AI, blockchain, crypto, and NFTs. While I can teach the legal limits of technology, it is the energy of students which carries this class, as they educate me.

In summary, I want my classes to not only be student-centered but life-centered as well.

Importance of the first day of class

My favorite moment of the semester is the first day of class. There's nothing like the anticipation of walking into a classroom on day one. To meet students for the first time and face the challenge of delivering a meaningful session. My students don't have time for nonsense; many are looking to graduate as quickly as they can. I assure them on day one that we will get them graduated in 20 years tops.

Sample 75-minute session

For me, the first day of class should be treated as an event. Something that students will enjoy and find out why this class will have relevance in their lives. These are typical student mindsets before I walk into class on day one:

"I'm here only because it's a required class."
"Law is boring!"
"Every section was closed except your 8:00 a.m. class."

Day one not only allows you to set the tone, but it also gives students the chance to size you up for the next few months. Thus, we must deliver something of value.

Before class, I place index cards on most desks. As students walk in closer to class time, I hand out additional cards. I have the first page of the syllabus displayed on the document camera or "doc cam." Handwritten at the top:

Index Cards

Name
Favorite movie or TV show dealing with LAW
What topic of law are you looking forward to learning about?

This is my icebreaker. I do this in class sizes ranging from 35–120 students. It gets students talking before the content. After I collect the cards, I start with:

"Welcome everyone to [fill in the class]. My name is Perry Binder and I'll give you my background after I meet each of you."

Then, one by one, I'll read the name and movie or TV show and topic of interest, with a chance for the student to elaborate. There is more than enough time in a 75-minute class to personally address each index card, up to 60 students. I'm unable to do that in classes of 120 students, but I'll still read aloud the movie or TV show from every index card. When I find interesting ones or ones I've never heard of, I'll look for those students and ask them questions.

In a class of 45 students, the icebreaker takes about 20 minutes. The real fun begins when some students walk into class late, as they likely had a tough time finding the classroom or a parking spot on campus. As a student awkwardly tries to slip in unnoticed, I'll say something like:

"Welcome to Chem 101—name three inert gases."

The panicked student looks around and then at me with confusion. Did I walk into the wrong room?

"Okay, two inert gases."

The students already in the room crack up. Instantly, that incoming student gets what's happening and is welcomed with a laugh. The next late student:

"Welcome to Geometry 101—State the Pythagorean Theorem."

And on and on it goes.

This hopefully signals to the class that there is potential to have fun here. All of this occurs before I even say a word about myself. Other than developing a rapport with students, I have an ulterior motive for the index card exercise, which unfolds all semester long: Hollywood portrays law cases that are neatly wrapped up in an hour or two, while the reality is much different. I attempt to demystify the legal process by showing how it is slow and easily manipulated, with mixed results for parties to a lawsuit.

A note on students who are late to class: I tell students I'd rather they walk in late than not show up at all. I have no idea what that person's day was like. Teachers have a lot of power, like a judge who can sanction an attorney for showing up late to court. I have seen judges abuse that power. I don't want to, and thus, I have no attendance or tardy policy.

Once I'm done with the index cards, I'll re-mention my name and give them my background, where I grew up, went to college and law school, where I practiced law, how I got into teaching, when I got to this institution, the classes I teach, and the interactions I have in the professional community. Next, I ask the following questions:

"Is this anyone's first semester at this college?"
"Is anyone here a graduating senior?"
"Is there anyone here who doesn't know one person in this room?"

To the first question, I offer a sincere welcome; for the second, I lead the class in a round of applause for those people; and for the third, I tell students that we are taking a five-minute break for you to speak with the individuals next to you, and maybe exchange contact information for notes missed in the future. The once-silent classroom becomes loud and joyous.

After the break, with the syllabus still on the doc cam, I go over its highlights, starting with how to contact me. I tell students that I am the easiest person on the planet to reach by email. When I get to class policies, here's one that we discuss:

Any and all opinions or statements as to legal matters made by the Instructor are for class discussion purposes only, and are never to be taken as dispensing legal advice. This includes any conversations during or outside of class time.

I probe the class on why I have this policy. Eventually, they figure out that I could be sued for malpractice if anything we discuss is considered legal advice and it is wrong, misapplied, or misunderstood. In addition, I tell students that my bar admission is from a different state and that technically if I gave legal advice here, it would be a misdemeanor for me, just like it would be for them. At that point, I announce an extra credit project:

"After class, go out on the quad, start giving legal advice, get arrested, go through the system, get convicted, and write it up in five pages—five points added to your first exam."

To date, I've had no takers. Next, I repeat very slowly and playfully:

"Don't call me if you are arrested!"

That statement launches into my best story of the semester (which you should use on the first day of class):

"I was in my office and I get a phone call from a student."
"Help me Perry, they're taking me awaaaaaaaaay!"
I'm like:
"Where the heck are youuuuuuuuuuuuuuuuu?"
"The DeKalb Detention Center."
"Yeah."

This story is told in its entirety in Appendix A.

Next, we discuss course expectations. I try to run my class like a law firm, with no micromanaging (see no attendance policy)—just get the job done. However, like a law firm, I am mostly unforgiving about project deadlines and missed exams, unless the student notifies me in advance with a valid excuse.

The syllabus emphasizes the importance of spelling and grammar in writing assignments. My favorite student error was the use of the word "faulty" instead of "faculty" member. Now, though, I'm wondering if that person got it right! Finally, I provide examples of awkward sentences and emphasize the importance of editing. See Appendix B for "Spelling/Grammatical Errors in Student Papers."

Make sure you "start class" on the first day

My class lasts 75 minutes, twice a week. On day one, the syllabus discussion, student in prison story, and index card icebreaker take about 40 minutes. Then we have 20 minutes of actual class content, with a promise that I'll get them out 15 minutes early as a first day gift.

Let's start class. My lectures are known for on-topic but exaggerated hand-drawn illustrations. I begin by displaying a ridiculous image and asking students to describe what they see.

After two minutes of wild guesses, disbelief, and laughter, I go over what happened in a case routinely discussed in first-year law school classes. I have students analyze the facts, predict who won, and assess why this court decision is important from a businessperson's perspective. They take notes, get the assignment for the next class, and then I send them packing.

If you are still guessing about the picture: A man is holding a package wrapped in newspaper. He is running to get on a slow moving train. The carriage door is still open, as the conductor attempts to pull the man aboard. Search *Palsgraf v. Long Island Railroad* for the rest of this crazy sequence of events.

For online courses, I upload .jpgs of my "Perry Doodles" to the learning management system. (LMS) During Zoom sessions, students guess in the chat what that day's comical picture depicts, and have a good laugh on me. Then, we discuss the connected concepts.

In summary, I try to make day one fun, interactive, and informative. I simulate how class is conducted and hope students are excited to come back for more.

Final thoughts on the first day of class

I am always looking to improve my teaching techniques. A few years ago, I observed the first day of class taught by four colleagues. Here are some ideas that I picked up:

1: Icebreaker: "If you were a superhero, which one would you be and why?" That was a great day one activity, though my response was lame. I said Spiderman because I'm the only one in my house unafraid of spiders.

2: One colleague wrapped up the introductions and syllabus in 15 minutes and then went directly into an interactive discussion on business ethics. Students were very engaged.

3: Another colleague posed these questions to a small class:
    - Where are you from?
    - What do expect from this class?
    - What do you want to do after college?
    - What has been your exposure to law?

That discussion lasted 45 minutes. Then, the professor projected a photograph of a chaotic car accident scene, and asked students what they think happened. They proceeded to assign liability among the parties. Fascinating.

4: A professor gave everyone a handout with several things going wrong in the professional life of a general manager. Students were then instructed to rank which event would produce the greatest legal exposure for the store. The class discussion was lively.

As you know, there are so many ways to make the first day of class memorable. My approach: Borrow from the best and put your unique spin on it.

CHAPTER 2

The Structure of Each In-Person and Online Class

While an icebreaker is critical for the first day of class, I believe in having an icebreaker for every class. I begin each session with a segment called "What's New in the Law News?" Outside of class, I read the news each day not just for important current law cases, but also for wacky or twisted cases or incidents. In the spirit of "less is truly more," all you need is a headline to spark a collective imagination. I print out the first page of articles and display the headlines on the doc cam with accompanying crazy photos:

- *Man being fired brings emotional support clown to meeting*
- *Teen taking train selfie kicked in head by conductor*
- *Woman fakes her own death to get out of bad online date*
- *Man stabbed at haunted house by friend who thought knife was a prop*
- *Rattlesnake, uranium, whiskey found at traffic stop*
- *Cop pulls over driver for speeding with 8,000-pound potato*

I keep a folder of these articles and reuse the best ones every semester. After I go through my items, I then say to the class:

"What did *you* find new in the law news?"

Some students are prepared to discuss a story. If no one participates, I say that I won't start class until I hear a few. They all have devices and we take time to look up things. This is my secret plan to get students to read the news instead of social media posts.

Many of you likely have an icebreaker or novel technique to start class. If you do, take notice of whether it gets you laughing and motivated to dive into whatever you are teaching. If not, look for ways to tweak it. Lean on the magic of collective laughter to get students excited about the day's lesson. In this regard, see Chapter 6: Help Students Stay Engaged Through Exaggeration and Humor.

To me, education at all levels is a two-way street. You get to impart knowledge to, instill hope in, and foster dreams for mostly eager students. In turn, they can elevate your mood and inspire your growth as an instructor and person.

There was a time when professors walked into a classroom early and students would talk with one another, read a newspaper, or look over the topics for the day. Those days disappeared in 2001 with the invention of the iPod, as students listened to their favorite songs. Today, walking into class is truly a moment of silence, with smartphones and EarPods engaged.

When I was in grade school, all of our teachers used white chalk on a green or black chalkboard. If they cut loose, maybe they had colorful chalk as well. The dusty erasers created quite a mess. Before the chalkboard made way for the whiteboard, the overhead projector was used, where a clear sheet of plastic would be placed on the machine, and what was written in magic marker was projected on a screen for viewing. This allowed teachers to face the class rather than write on the board. Plus, they could prepare material in advance rather than get to class early and jot things on the board. In college, I had an Economics professor who drew fancy graphs on an overhead projector with scrolling clear plastic. I briefly used the overhead to go over exams in class. It required the hassle of photocopying the exam on clear sheets.

For me, the greatest classroom invention was the Elmo projector which gave me the freedom to display exams, newspaper articles, and textbook passages. Today, we use many versions of this doc cam.

At some point, computers made their way to a teacher's classroom desk. In the days before cellphones and other devices, oftentimes I would get to class early and students were on the teacher's computer, logging in to check their email. Even if they had a laptop, there was a time when wireless service didn't exist. Back then, the internet worked by connecting the device with an ethernet, and most classrooms didn't have ports for every seat.

Obviously, computers in the classroom gave teachers the ability to show PowerPoint slides. I don't use PowerPoint. Sure, I use it at academic conferences and corporate presentations because it is slick and expected, but I'm of the (minority?) opinion that it is not the optimal tool for learning.

I'm not here to change your mind; just here to give another perspective. My method might be similar to your use of PowerPoint, if your slides are skeletal, with three or four words and an image. The PowerPoint presentations with full sentences, definitions, and examples are the ones that I don't find effective because students are just reading along as you are talking. I know that many students want those kinds of slides uploaded to the university's LMS, so they have a full set of notes. In fact, I'll get the occasional negative comment on student reviews:

"He doesn't use PowerPoint!"

I believe in honing listening skills through note-taking. I won't cite research that shows that writing things down reinforces learning. Conversely, I won't object to your retort that many students are visual learners and need PowerPoint.

My method supports visual learning, as I place "term sheets" and concept-connected images on the doc cam. The term sheets are pre-loaded in Word on the LMS. This gives students with laptops the ability to type notes directly onto the document. In the old days, I handed out paper copies.

I developed this style long ago when freshmen and sophomores would ask me:

"When is the study guide going to be out for the first exam?"

They were accustomed to getting these course aids from many of their high school teachers. Students use my term sheets to create a study guide by listening and taking notes in class. I provide a sample in Appendix C.

During class, I write things directly on the term sheet, which students see on the doc cam. When we review for exams, students see all of these markings again, as they ask questions on each page. Some will take a photo with their phone, though my scratch appears chaotic and is far short of a full set of notes. During the review, if people ask me to fill in a blank, I know that they never attended that particular class.

"Flipping" a class

In 2014, I taught a four-plus hour MBA class each week but needed to be out of town on a particular date. Rather than burdening a colleague to handle that much material as a substitute, I recorded a 75-minute video in an empty classroom. The instructor was seen in a small corner box while the term sheet on the doc cam took up the rest of the viewing screen.

Students were required to watch that, as well as an actual trial video before class. Then, I assigned interactive class modules (see Chapter 3) for students to read. The beauty of this experiment was that students needed to show up for only two, rather than four hours of class. Likewise, a colleague who covered for me was there for half the time, did not need to "lecture," and was available to answer questions and guide the class through the modules. I wrote a pedagogy article about this experience, which can be read online:

> Perry Binder, *Flipping a Law Class Session: Creating Effective Online Content and Real World In-Class Team Modules*, 17 ATLANTIC LAW JOURNAL 34–69 (2015). *Atlanticlawjournal.org*

The seeds were planted for me to eventually flip an entire course. During the pandemic, I recorded numerous podcasts which tracked the term sheets. When we returned to face-to-face classes in Fall 2021, I assigned all of them for students to listen to and take notes before class. Instead of re-lecturing in the classroom, I answered questions on the material, re-explained difficult concepts, added new material, and (in my mind), successfully flipped the class with interactive exercises. At least one student was awake in the 8:00 a.m. section. That person enthusiastically approved of the format in an anonymous course evaluation:

"I didn't think a real life teacher could pull off a flipped class but good [*****] job my dude."

In January 2022, the Omicron variant was raging and many face-to-face students were unable to attend class in person; thus, I permitted students to attend from home via Zoom. The main drawback was that they were unable to see items displayed on the doc cam. However, since they had the term sheets, virtual students were able to follow along. I'd estimate about twenty percent of the class attended remotely. Aside from COVID concerns, most of my students commute and have part- or full-time jobs, so virtual attendance provides some relief in managing their daily challenges. At times, commuters attend class on smartphones via Zoom—when stuck in parking lots or stranded on the road:

"I thought I'd have to drop the class or be very late every week because of limited parking."

"My car broke down ... and I'm still sitting in the car waiting for help on the side of the road."

My Zoom account permits unlimited usage for up to 100 people. Since I move around the room a lot, I carry my lightweight work-issued laptop and occasionally peek at the chat for comments. If someone in person asks a question, I'll repeat it for those attending remotely. Even group activities can be done virtually, as students are instructed to chat online for solutions.

A few notes on in-person/simulcast classes:

- Our MBA classrooms have a fancy simulcast feature, so remote students can see everything in the classroom, including the doc cam.
- Students in my face-to-face classes are required to take exams in person.
- A dual virtual/in-person environment is challenging when going over an exam after students receive their grades. I don't allow those in the classroom to photograph my test displayed on the doc cam. My rule is that all devices, laptops, etc. need to be down during the discussion. When I go over the MBA exam, I turn off the simulcast video feed and only have audio on. Thus, students are highly encouraged to attend this session in person.

Online Classes—Replicating the In-Person Experience

While the majority of my teaching is in-person, I have taught online classes since 2001. Back then, we relied greatly on discussion boards. Synchronous (or live) chat sessions were first conducted by typing in the chat feature; then we graduated to audio chats, and finally to audiovisual. Certainly, the pandemic thrust all college instructors into the online class world. In March 2020, our university was closed for two weeks. In that time, we needed to figure out how to transition from face-to-face classes to an online format. Still in a daze, I discovered Zoom, relied on tech support, and was asked to assume a Digital Hero role to assist faculty who had never taught online.

Today, my online classes are synchronous. The college sets a designated class time and students attend live virtual meetings after listening to my podcast on that week's topic. Many professors teach asynchronously. For example, students listen to instructor podcasts, complete assigned tasks, and respond to items on discussion boards. The main benefit of asynchronous classes is that they permit participants to complete assignments at their own pace, without tying them to a "show up" time.

I run my online class just as I do the in-person class. Anything I might place on the doc cam when students are in-person, I share with online students. For example, with "What's New in the Law News," I put headlines and attendant photos on a Word document and share them one by one. To me, we miss the synergy of students socializing and networking, and at times it's hard to manage an online class when five students raise their hands to speak. However, I have adjusted by using the chat at times to gauge their understanding of the material and to see if they posted questions for me.

I do not record my synchronous sessions for two reasons:

1. I don't want to have a record of sensitive ethical and legal questions discussed; and
2. I am protective of my intellectual property.

To the first point, I want students to speak freely. To the second, I am guarded about having my analysis of the material "out there." While I record several podcasts, they are factual, follow the course content, and do not have my insights on the particular subjects. (which I provide in the live sessions) My syllabus states:

> For privacy and intellectual property reasons, I do not record Zoom sessions and you are not permitted to do so. All class notes and lectures, whether in person, print, video, or otherwise, are the IP of the Instructor and may not be used or distributed in any form without the written permission of the Instructor. You may not record or photograph the class without the Instructor's permission, and you may not post, disseminate, sell, license, or file-share any such recording or image to any other person, company, entity, file-share service, or otherwise. Materials displayed, posted, or distributed in this class are for class use and *your* learning only. The copyright to all original class materials is owned by the Instructor.

When my college had a Professional MBA program, we were required to record in-person sessions on our LMS platform. I complied with this policy but would always pause the recording when we got to sensitive ethical issues. I recognize that as we eventually teach online classes on a global basis with students from different time zones, I will need to record live sessions or teach asynchronously. That day isn't upon me. Yet.

CHAPTER 3

Using AI to Enhance Classroom Activities and Student Projects

Like many of you, I am constantly reading articles to understand generative artificial intelligence and its impact on teaching and learning. Tools such as Bard, ChatGPT, and DALL·E are being used in diverse fields, as these headlines suggest:

- *7 Ways Creatives Use AI in Art and Design*
- *ChatGPT was Able to Give Better Medical Advice on Depression than Real Doctors, New Study Shows*

In mid-2023, I conducted an anonymous student survey about AI:

1: Have you ever used an AI tool such as ChatGPT?
Yes 15 / No 16

2: Have you ever used AI for a job?
Yes 4 / No 27

3: Have any of your professors assigned a project where you needed to use an AI tool?
Yes 1 / No 30

4: Have you ever used an AI tool for a class assignment without a professor's permission?
Yes 6 / No 25

Anticipating that these numbers will increase over time, I decided to experiment with AI. Below are examples of my use of ChatGPT in creating or updating student assignments.

For every course, I use real world classroom activities and outside-of-class projects. The goals for each exercise are to apply the material taught, promote critical thinking, and encourage student interaction.

In-Class Activities

Some of my modules are based on actual cases I had when practicing law. Students are pushed to figure out solutions to complicated legal and ethical questions when challenged by fact-shifting scenarios. To foster problem-solving skills, participants are told that some of the modules are intentionally written vaguely to generate a wide range of reactions and solutions.

These in-class activities require little to no prior student preparation. They are designed to have them break into small groups to discuss and reconvene as a class for analysis. The amount of time depends on the complexity of the facts. The information drawn from these exercises is testable. Appendix D has a sample module that I created before experimenting with AI:

> *Products Liability & Ethics Module.* Students are required to watch a video of an actual trial outside of class time, and then in class, answer several questions that are connected to information learned in the unit.

One semester, I experimented with my MBA class, by requiring prior preparation for modules. I assigned ungraded weekly material where rotating student teams had to prepare a short memorandum, upload it to the course's LMS, email it to me, and lead a class discussion. I provided written feedback on the memo before the class session. My intent was for students to have a folder of executive memos without the burden of each team doing the work every week. Many people complained about two things:

1. *Why are we writing this if you're not grading them?* My students get annoyed when asked to hand in work untied to a grade.
2. *Some of the modules are more involved than others, so it's unfair for us.* True, which is why I didn't grade them. However, the disparity in work was not stark.

In the end, I decided not to assign modules like that again because of the unequal student work distribution and the unneeded aggravation. Live, learn, and listen to students.

Using artificial intelligence to create modules is a work in progress. First, I needed to become proficient in writing "prompts" or targeted phrases to type in an AI platform. Then I had to determine the topics within the curriculum to experiment with. For example, in Fall 2023, I turned to AI to help me create modules for my Consumer Law class. Using a free tool, ChatGPT 3.5, I posed the following prompts:

- List each step of what to do if your identity is stolen;
- What do you do if your bank account is wrongfully garnished (frozen) by a creditor with a judgment?; and
- What steps would you take if you paid a mechanic for repairs, the car still does not work, and the mechanic wants to charge you more money?

I asked the class to break into groups of two or three for five minutes to discuss what they would do in the above situations. When we reconvened, I went around the room for their thoughts. Finally, I put the AI-generated responses on the doc cam and we compared what the students said and what ChatGPT produced. Then I weighed in on where I think the students and AI did well and what I might suggest doing differently. The conversation was lively and demonstrated the accuracy and possible flaws of relying on AI.

Another example involved a class discussion on mediation (where a trained facilitator assists parties in resolving a civil dispute) in preparation for our mock mediation session. In such exercises, typically everyone is provided with a common set of facts, and separate confidential facts are given to the plaintiff and defendant.

In the past, it took me several hours to develop one fact pattern for this activity. By using AI, I generated a practice scenario in a matter of minutes. To begin, I entered a general prompt, "mediation simulation scenario," which generated a 150-word fact pattern involving a landlord-tenant disagreement. Then I typed in "fair compromise for mediation simulation" and hit the "Regenerate Response" button twice. That gave me three options for AI's solution to choose from to share with the class. Weeks later, I determined that the scenario needed more specificity. I added a few of my own common facts and confidential facts for each side of the disagreement. My lack of foresight to do so while generating the original fact pattern taught me a lesson in making sure I did a thorough job of anticipating all of the prompts needed to make a simulation and class discussion more realistic.

With AI's work and my minor touches, I produced a very organized set of common facts, unique positions for each side, and a fair compromise solution. After the mock session, the students and I assessed how the mediation played out and discussed fair compromises for each party. Then we compared and contrasted these thoughts with the solutions generated by AI. See Appendix E for the landlord-tenant prompts, fact pattern, the compromise solutions, and my additional facts.

To me, the great thing about AI is how I can create activities quickly, sensitize students to the positive uses and limitations of AI, and develop students' critical thinking skills by creating solutions on their own and then testing how those solutions measure up to AI's answers.

Individual Projects

Recently, I used AI for an assignment requiring students to write a detailed demand letter. (a professional letter detailing a dispute with someone or a company, asserting legal rights, and laying out a demand for recourse) In the past, this task took students a few hours to write a great letter. Predicting that lawyers and consumer advocates would soon use AI to complete this type of work, I demonstrated to Consumer Law students how to create a demand letter using AI. Ideally, they needed to recall an actual civil dispute in their lives (if not, make one up) and generate a professional letter.

Learning my lesson to envision all facts while using ChatGPT 3.5, these are the chronological prompts I used to create a "made up" demand letter:

- *Write demand letter landlord in Atlanta won't fix air conditioning*
- *Add six dates over a ten day period that tenant called or emailed landlord*
- *Now put those dates in the body of the demand letter*
- *Add in May 4: I got three estimates from a repair company attached to this letter*

  - Did not do it

  - I then hit the Regenerate button which got it done

- *Use real names John Smith is the tenant Jill Jones is the landlord*

  - It did it!

- *Now add a statement at the end if I do not hear back by May 12 hire third party under repair and deduct law*

  I gave students constructive feedback on their letters but did not grade them; after all, they didn't write them! Instead, I incorporated this activity into a graded assignment, which included:

Project Based on Demand Letter

Part I: Revise your Demand Letter per my feedback and upload it with Parts II & III. (the revised letter will be graded)

To read my AI-generated demand letter and full assignment, see Appendices F and G, respectively.

Testing the limits of AI, I experimented with whether ChatGPT 3.5 could produce a simple small claims court complaint based on the facts contained in the made up demand letter. While it generated the facts accurately and numbered each allegation, it had formatting and other issues that rendered this idea unusable for our purposes. Instead, the assignment morphed into having students fill out a county small claims court template in Word, as any consumer would who didn't know how to write a complaint. Perhaps this task is doable in a later version of ChatGPT or with other tools. Ultimately, AI will be an important time-saving feature, as lawyers and consumer advocates tailor forms to avoid "reinventing the wheel."

In other courses, I determined that my old assignments could easily be completed by students using AI without my knowledge. Anticipating this, I changed the instructions by requiring students to use AI in a limited fashion, coupled with a reflection component. Below is a portion of an assignment for my Internet Law class.

How the Internet Changed Professions

<u>Understatement</u>: The internet has changed how we do business, whether in the United States or worldwide.

Section A. Use a free AI tool (I use the free version of ChatGPT 3.5)—figure out what prompt to use. Choose ANY profession. Discuss how the internet has improved, complicated, revolutionized, and/or adversely impacted the profession and the people working in that profession. (500–700-ish words)

To read the full assignment including two AI-generated responses to Section A above, a reflection component in Section B, and a research requirement in Section C, see Appendix H, "Incorporating AI with Minor Tweak to Assignment." Alternatively, the above assignment can be easily converted to a shorter extra credit paper by removing the research component.

Team Projects

In 2019, I taught Consumer Law for the first time and unknowingly set the bar too high when it came to assigning a team project. I had students write a demand or response letter from scratch, draft an actual Complaint or Answer, and argue a case before a simulated small claims court judge. (me) We spent many hours in class learning how to do these tasks. While the letters were well written and the trials were a success, the quality of the Complaints and Answers was not up to par. I had asked too much of them, expecting that they could replicate court pleadings with complex forms and my instructions. I apologized to them and did not grade that work harshly. Instead, I wrote a model Complaint and Answer for the teams to use at their trials. For the 2020 team project, I shifted gears by providing very easy small claims court Complaint and Answer forms to fill out.

As you already know, some projects don't work well the first time. I think it's important to admit mistakes to students and adjust on the fly. Beginning in 2021, I converted the team assignment to the individual project previously discussed and conducted the mock mediation and trials as a fun extra credit assignment.

At the MBA level, we are encouraged by the college to assign graded group projects to simulate workplace dynamics. In Appendix I, I provide an exercise entitled "Discovery Ethics and

Attorney-Client Privilege Project." Student teams are placed in the role of a manager and told to gather documents for a lawsuit filed against the company. That manager is told by the supervisor to destroy a relevant but damaging document, which forces students to navigate uncomfortable workplace issues.

My project grading method is included in Appendix I. Though untied to the grade, I try to hold students accountable for their work by having team members separately evaluate each group member's contribution, as well as their own. Only the instructor reads what each student wrote. This "Team Project Peer Evaluation Form" is available in Appendix J.

Next semester, I am thinking of ideas to incorporate AI into team projects. For the MBA project above, one easy tweak would be to have students use AI to research what is needed for the attorney-client privilege to apply in the corporate context during the discovery process of a lawsuit. Then I would ask the team to compare what we learned in class and analyze whether AI's response was accurate.

My use of AI detailed in this chapter is rudimentary and easily adaptable to your activities and projects. Here are some basic tips on writing prompts:*

- Be specific;
- Use context (help the tool understand the nuance behind your question);
- Ask open-ended questions for detailed responses; and
- Be direct and concise.

I am excited to learn about more sophisticated uses of AI in

---

* Source: Roland Hutchinson, *How to write better ChatGPT prompts*, GEEKY GADGETS (Oct. 17, 2023).

higher education and intend to continue experimenting with groundbreaking tools.

A final note on AI, which is beyond the scope of this book. Advances in technology usually raise novel legal issues and it takes courts and legislative bodies several years to keep up. For example, as this book goes to press, lawsuits have been filed by high-profile authors claiming copyright infringement of their works by AI companies, as the latter's tools are "learning" from these works and generating derivative material without permission. Time will tell how the courts will rule on the use of this game-changing technology.

CHAPTER 4

Preparing Students for Multiple Choice and Essay Exams

You and I know how difficult it is to write challenging and objective exams covering all of the important material. Some of our multiple choice questions are too easy, and grading certain essay responses might be too subjective.

Before each undergraduate exam, I devote an entire class period to a Unit review. Prior to the first exam, I give students advice on what to expect on my tests and give them sample questions with model answers. The three types of questions that I use are straightforward multiple choice questions, application multiple choice questions, and essays.

For closed-note exams, students should prepare flashcards on index cards for each of my terms. Alternatively, I encourage students to look up my name and course on Quizlet, since former students have created online flashcards here. I find some errors but in general, they are at least 95-plus percent accurate.

The flashcard system works well for straightforward multiple choice questions. However, many questions involve the application of concepts, not the mere memorization of material. One way to prepare for such questions is to study and discuss course material with a fellow student. I explain to them that a well-written college exam question will make you think critically about the course material. On open-note exams, I only use application multiple choice questions.

Sample straightforward multiple choice question

Harold Homeowner didn't like having the neighborhood teenagers walk across his yard every night. So he dug a huge hole on his lawn, along the path the teens usually take. Then he placed a bear trap at the bottom of the hole and cleverly covered it with tree branches and leaves. One night while walking across Harold's property, Tim fell in, got caught in the bear trap, and was seriously injured. The next morning, Harold went out for the newspaper and to see what he'd caught. Tim screamed: "My leg. I'm hurt!" In Tim's lawsuit for injuries, Harold will likely:

a. win because Tim was a trespasser and landowners owe no duty to trespassers. Harold could even surround his home with a moat filled with water and alligators to make sure Tim stays off his freshly cut lawn.

b. lose because landowners owe a duty to keep the premises free from unreasonable dangers they create for trespassers.

I know which answer you'd like to pick. Choose the other one for exam purposes.

Sample application multiple choice question

This morning on the way to his exam at a university in our state, Marcel purchased coffee at the drive-through window of a local burger establishment. With the car stopped, he placed the cup between his knees and opened the lid to add cream. Accidentally, he knocked the contents of the cup onto his lap, and hot coffee soaked through his sweatpants. He screamed: "Help me, I'm burning, and I've got a test in 20 minutes!" Marcel headed straight to the hospital, where doctors treated his third-degree burns. He then sued the burger joint for failing to warn him that extremely hot coffee can rip through flesh. A jury awarded Marcel $100,000 in damages. It also found him to be 75% responsible and the defendant 25% responsible for the accident. How much money would Marcel be permitted to recover if the defendant does not appeal this verdict?

    a. $100,000
    b. $75,000
    c. $25,000
    d. $0

Answering the above question requires a three-step process:

1. Understanding the legal concept of "comparative negligence";
2. Calculating simple numbers; and
3. Applying a state rule for comparative negligence.

If you chose the incorrect letter "c," at least you partially understand the legal concept of comparative negligence in my state. Under this legal principle, a plaintiff's award is reduced by the percentage of fault assigned by the jury for an accident. However, in many states, if a plaintiff is found to be 50% or more responsible, then that plaintiff would recover nothing from the $100,000 verdict. Thus, the correct response for those states would be the letter "d." Moral of the story: Know your state laws!

If an exam has a mixture of multiple choice and essay questions, I tell students to take a brief look at the latter to gauge how much time might be needed, but to do the multiple choice first. Don't dwell on a few questions for long periods of time.

On open-note exams, I warn students that they will run out of time if they spend too much time searching through notes. Better to put a mark next to a confusing question, work efficiently through the exam, and go back to the difficult ones at the end.

Essay Exams

Here's what I tell students about essay exams: Ask your professor beforehand if you can write answers in an "essay outline" format. Except for open-ended questions, they are usually looking for some specific responses, so underline the key terms. This method will draw professors to your most important points in an organized and efficient manner. It will also make professors happy because the essay will be easier to grade. See Appendix K for a "Sample Essay Exam Question and Model Answer." The Answer is written in an essay outline format.

Open-Note Exams

Students have complained to me for years about closed-note exams. It only took a pandemic for me to think about this.

I cannot recall giving an open-note exam in face-to-face classes. However, in Fall 2021, as a way to transition students back to in-person instruction, I permitted students to bring in any paper notes and the textbook. In addition, they could access the LMS but not the internet. (which wouldn't help much anyway because most of my multiple choice questions are application questions)

Students appreciated that I provided a Word document of the term sheets in the LMS so they could utilize the Control F function and go straight to a term. Before the exam, I advised them to re-listen to my podcasts, fill in any missing notes, and examine the material as it applies to the business world. The results for Exam 1 in Spring 2022 for two classes were similar to my typical closed-note exam statistics:

Undergraduate Exam 1 (includes a 6-point curve)
90+ = 15 students
80+ = 17 students
70+= 18 students
Under 70= 18 students

Takeaways: By listening to students, I did away with closed-note exams and thus, with most straightforward multiple choice questions which require rote memorization. Students must use critical thinking skills to apply legal concepts to application multiple choice questions and work efficiently so they do not run out of the allotted exam time. To date, I am still using the open-note exam format. However, there are drawbacks to permitting the use of devices such as the potential for cheating (unauthorized use of the internet), loss of wireless connections to access the LMS, and drained laptop batteries. In the future, I will likely simplify the format by eliminating the use of all devices but permitting students to bring one or two pages of typed or handwritten notes to exams.

My exam gift for graduating seniors

When I was in college, some professors gave graduating seniors the choice to opt out of the final exam. Senioritis set in and I always appreciated the gesture. I adopted that gift idea for my undergraduate seniors. See Appendix L for how I calculate senior course grades.

My law school graduation reality check "gift"

College graduation was a fun day for me. I had a good time sitting with my classmates. Law school graduation didn't have the same vibe but I went and listened to the speakers with one ear on them and the other on my friends. The keynoter was a well-respected state appellate court judge. She spoke about the honor of becoming an attorney and the importance of ethics. Then she said in a slow, steady, and booming voice:

"You think you've taken your last test??!!"

That quickly got my attention, as my eyes locked on hers. I figured she was referring to the upcoming state bar exam, which is the reason law school graduation didn't have the same exuberant feeling as college graduation. She pointed her crooked finger at the grads and continued in a methodical tone:

"Eeeeeeeevery day you walk into my courtroom will be a test."

Talk about sucking the life out of a joyous day!

CHAPTER 5

Teach to Your Strengths

In stressful moments, lean on your strengths. I learned this lesson on day one of the first class I ever taught, Introduction to American Government. I thought that we should start class at the very beginning of the textbook, with a discussion of the Founding Fathers and the Federalist Papers. As I was speaking, I repeatedly said to myself:

"You don't know anything about this topic beyond what you read last night."

After forty-five minutes of panic, sweat, and utter confusion, we took a ten-minute break. In that time, I decided to go straight to the Bill of Rights, a topic of strength. The rest of the session thankfully went more smoothly.

It is very important for me to be honest with students about what areas of law I know well and what areas I have no experience with, beyond researching the subject matter. I practiced law as a business litigator, which means I saw diverse commercial cases go to court from the plaintiff's and defendant's sides. While I know a lot about most intellectual property concerns—copyrights, trademarks, and trade secrets—I would not be able to competently explain how to write a patent application. I never practiced family law or estate law. And my only criminal law exposure is in dealing with traffic tickets and students locked up wrongfully.

I bring this up because the more honest we are with students, the more they will trust us. They also get to learn that lawyers are specialists and that businesspeople need to reach out to attorneys who have practiced in a particular area. If a student asks a really good question in class but I don't know the answer, I'll say "Send me an email and I'll look it up." Just like lawyers, teachers don't need to know everything—they just need to know how to research subject-related information.

Oh yeah, forget strengths for a second. First, figure out how to compensate for your weaknesses. One of my glaring weaknesses as a professor is an inability to remember student names or recognize their faces outside of class. One time, just before class started, a student walked up to me and said:

"I saw you on campus yesterday, and you didn't even say 'hi.' That was rude!"

I desperately tried to explain that names and faces are hard for me to recall in a class with 120 students.

So now, when I walk around a college with 50,000 students, I'm compelled to wave hello to everyone I make eye contact with.

"Hi, how goes it?!"

Four out of five of them are looking at me, like:

"Do I know you?"

But that fifth person, the one I should know, appreciates the hello. So now I'm walking, smiling, waving, and babbling. All over campus.

Aside from leaning on your academic strengths, figuring out how to adjust to unexpected classroom situations is a strength that can give you confidence and reassurance as a teacher.

Adapting on the fly

I guarantee that K–12 teachers have much better stories than me on the ability to adapt on the fly in the classroom. Whenever I meet teachers, I tell them that they are my personal heroes for educating our youth and for dealing with sometimes chaotic days. If middle or high school teachers say that some techniques in this book would not work in class, I'll listen intently and defer to their experience.

I had to adapt on the fly in Fall 2020 for a previously referenced Consumer Law project, culminating in a trial at the end of the semester. Four groups of plaintiffs and four groups of defendants for four mini-trials, with yours truly as the judge.

Meeting together in person is the most effective way to accomplish this task. However, COVID necessitated that many students meet virtually. Still, I was determined to make this work:

> The trials were conducted in a face-to-face class session. While participation in the trial was mandatory, the Instructor feared that many students would be unable to attend for health or work-related reasons. Thus, students were given a choice to attend the trial in-person or via Zoom. The virtual session proved to be challenging but somewhat manageable. ... The students attending in person were required to bring their laptops and log into Zoom so the entire class was together. At times, this dynamic created an echo effect on the computers when someone spoke in the classroom. In terms of introducing documents into evidence, students and the Instructor transitioned between the document camera for people in the classroom and the 'share' function of Zoom for remote participants.*

Of the students participating, fourteen attended in person and fourteen attended via Zoom.

As instructors, we learn how to adjust on the fly and hope that the outcome is adequate. I wouldn't say that the half-in-person/half-Zoom experiment was a success, but it got us through the required assignment.

---

* Excerpt: Perry Binder, *Teaching Consumer Law & Advocacy Skills with a Judge Judy Team Project*, 31 MIDWEST L.J. 27–60, 35 (Fall 2021)

CHAPTER 6

HELP STUDENTS ENGAGE THROUGH EXAGGERATION AND HUMOR

In Chapter 1, you caught a glimpse of my gifted artistic talent. (train conductor, passenger, ring a bell?) Throughout the semester, I introduce main topics with hand-drawn pictures. For example, to begin the intellectual property material, I'll ask the class what patented invention is displayed below:

Incredulous students guess what the absurd picture is and it becomes a fun vehicle to generate discussion. If you must know what this invention is, go to the bottom of Appendix C, the intellectual property term sheet. And no, it is not a flying saucer. That would be silly.

Classrooms give me the freedom to do things I couldn't do in courtrooms—be myself. In class, if I want to jump on a table or answer a student's cell phone, it's not only acceptable but happily taken in by the class. Hey, when MY phone rang in class once, the students got to answer it. Do you think a judge would tolerate this behavior?

My style is one of improvisation. The material is set, but the atmosphere is to expect the unexpected. I actually welcome distractions and discovered that they help students stay focused. When their minds are wandering, I need something to bring them back on track. One time, the class was nervous about an exam, so I asked a student to stand up as I gave her my whiteboard marker. I then ran to the front of the classroom with my back to the students, and instructed her to wing the marker at my head —missed me, wide right. Another time I wore a pair of Sketchers to class but was skeptical about how they looked. I asked for student opinions by jumping on the computer console table and placing a sole on the doc cam, which projected an Imax theater-size image.

Below are some illustrations of using exaggeration and humor to emphasize a point in class.

Sometimes, life can be murder—or not

My state legislature passed this bill:

> **Right to Self-Defense Act**
>
> A person is justified in threatening or using force against another and <u>does not have a duty to retreat</u> when and to the extent that he or she <u>reasonably believes</u> that such threat or force is necessary to defend himself or herself or a third person against such other's imminent use of unlawful force.
>
> <u>Class hypothetical</u>: You are in a city park in the daylight hours and there is a person 200 feet away. He is limping slowly towards

you with a walking cane in one hand and a big old axe in the other. He yells:

"I'm gonna cut you up and feed you to the pigeons."

You are wearing your running shoes and compete for the university's track team. You also happen to lawfully possess a gun on your person.

Many states have a self-defense law that says you have a duty to try and get away if faced with this situation. The above law eliminates the duty to retreat from another person's force, even if able to do so.

In my hypothetical, wouldn't it be wise to haul on out of there? However, if there is no duty to retreat, I guess the possibilities are endless:

> You: Well hello there, Mr. Limping Crazy Man wielding a lumberman's axe. Your blade looks mighty sharp and shiny.
> Him: Why yes, better to slice you to ribbons.
> You: Hang on a second as I live stream this on my phone.
> Him: Did they give you a rebate on that device? Hey, by the way, my name is Johnny. Heerrrre's Johnny!
> (*The Shining* movie reference)
> You: Great. Come a drop closer. And by the way: Say hello to my little friend! (*Scarface*)

Sometimes humor and exaggeration are needed to teach a very serious and sensitive legal topic. If zealous district attorneys wish to prosecute you for shooting Limping Crazy Man, they will need to show that you did not act reasonably. What does the phrase "reasonably believes" mean in the above law? That's a question for the jury as to whether your act constituted self-defense.

Finally, I tell students the most important thing to remember if you're sitting in jail accused of homicide in this scenario—THE very, very, very most important thing to remember (students leaning in now) is to never, EVER say:

"Uh, Professor Binder said it would be okay if I did this."

Laughter is the best medicine

I always dread giving back the first exam of the semester, since it is the first time students might get negative feedback in the course. So after going over the test, we usually take a break, and then I need to use my best material.

As we begin the Contracts unit, I start by asking the class whether anyone has been to a pawn shop. But I ask in my New York accent because the word "pawn" in New Yorkese sounds like "porn."

"Who here has been to a 'porn' shop?"

Three hands shoot up from the back row—yeah, me! Uneasiness and mild laughter follow.

"Come on, who here's been in a 'porn' shop?"

Disbelief and murmurs all around. Finally, someone is bold enough to ask in a proper Southern accent:

"Do you mean a paaawwwwn shop?"

"I'm like, yeah, a 'porn' shop." (playing innocent)

Raucous laughter fills the room.

"What?"

"It's paaawwwwwn shop."

Then they ask how I say porn and pawn.

"Porn. And 'porn.'"

From there, we go on to discuss a case dealing with contracts and a title paaawwwn shop. The day still stinks for those who received poor grades, but hopefully, comic relief helped.

Lay low, very low, in the weeds

Every semester, I ask my students if they've ever lent money to a boyfriend or girlfriend, but never got repaid. Some hands go up. This leads to a discussion on promissory notes. Then with trepidation, I ask if anyone's ever heard the scariest words on the planet:

"If you love me..."

If you do, don't immediately run. Wait for the rest of the sentence, presented to you from best to worst case scenario:

"If you love me, you'll help with the laundry."
"If you love me, you'll pull that bank heist for me."
"If you love me, you'll get rid of the decaying body in the trunk of my car."
"If you love me, you'll loan me some more money."

Listen, assess, and dive quickly into the weeds as needed.

Company lawyers think we are really stupid

I found these product warnings on the internet (so they must be true):

- Package of peanuts: Warning: Contains nuts
- Chainsaw: Do not stop chain with your hands
- Kitchen knife: Keep out of children
- Clothing iron: Do not iron clothes on body*

    * Some people in class usually admit that they have done this!

Sometimes people don't always know when you're joking

Actual questions that students have asked me in class:

"Are you a member of an organized crime family?"
"Are you really in the witness protection program?"
"Have you ever killed someone?"
"Why do hot dogs come in packs of 10 and buns in 8?"

I learn a lot by watching other professors teach their classes. Borrowing from others facilitates growth as a teacher, but you know what works best for you better than anyone. If it fits your teaching style, help students engage through exaggeration and humor.

CHAPTER 7

How I Got Here

I never dreamed of being a college professor. Does anybody?

As a kid, I was convinced that I would be playing basketball in Madison Square Garden for the Knicks. When it became obvious that my footwork wasn't quick enough, I figured I better get my brain to work a little harder. I graduated from high school at 16, college at 20, and law school at 23. I was on the fast track.

I gave my elementary school teachers fits, as evidenced by my report cards:

Second Grade: Improvement needed in self-control
Fourth Grade: Perry needs to exert more self-control
Sixth Grade: Perry needs to exercise better self-control

Psychologists will tell you that the best predictor of future behavior is past behavior. How then did this misfit wind up in a classroom, the very scene of his childhood transgressions?

At age 23, I was eager to start my law career. In court, I looked like I was 11. Maybe 16 with a suit and tie. Most opposing counsel perceived my youthful appearance as an invitation to bully an unseasoned attorney. In one case, I was having a hard time with a crusty and sketchy lawyer, "Sal," who defended a company that owed my client money. In civil law cases, attorneys are allowed to seek information from the other side in the "discovery" phase of the lawsuit. As was my typical practice, I sent a notice for the other side to produce documents, so I could analyze them and prepare for a deposition of the defendant.

Perry Binder

Only, this guy played games and never produced the documents or made his client available for a sworn statement. Each time we set the deposition, they never appeared. Sal abused the discovery process, and we had to run to the judge every time to make him comply. This took several court appearances and wasted time and my client's money.

Finally, I got Sal into our huge conference room. You've seen them in the movies: garish artwork, an obscenely long mahogany table, and fancy high back leather chairs. Joining me was the court reporter to transcribe the event, and "Larry," our firm's law clerk who was attending a local law school.

Sal and his client walked in late. As he flung the documents at me, he barked:

"Start the deposition!"

I calmly told him that Larry and I needed some time to look over the docs before beginning.

"Start the depo or we're outta here!"

Blah. Blah. Blah.

After some more yelling and whining, we started the deposition, where Sal's client was required to answer questions under oath. Sal objected to almost every question and we go at it. Back and forth, up and down, your mother, my mother, you mutha. Finally, he leaned across the massive table, stared me down, and blathered:

"I've been in this business too long to be pushed around by a young punk like you."

Okay. This was getting good. The court reporter worked it into the record. I guess I needed to say something, as I sniffed my leather chair:

"Yeah."

The court reporter shoots a look at me of "Really?" I tried again.

"Yeah. You're right, you have been in this business too long and it's about time we clean it up!"

Not bad, I'm thinking. Maybe a 6 out of 10 on comebacks. Well, whatever I said, Sal just snapped. He forklifted that huge ol' body out of his chair and started waddling around the long table, coming at me like the Penguin on *Batman*. All he needed was an umbrella:

"I've never hit an attorney, but I'm gonna hit you now!"

The court reporter's smile widened, as she kept on typing.

Meanwhile, I just sat in my high back, half-amused as Sal made his way toward me. Suddenly, Larry sprung out of his chair and jumped in front of me as Sal approached. Larry assumed the *Karate Kid* Crane Technique stance to ward off this looney lawyer. Sal waved his fist, so Larry started flapping his wings.

Not much surprises me, but this one's way up there. I just turned to the court reporter and said:

"Let the record reflect that opposing counsel waddled halfway around the room and threatened me with verbal and physical violence." (And that Larry's getting a good letter of recommendation from me.)

Okay, maybe Larry wasn't exactly in the Crane position, but they should really teach that move in law school.

Waddling Weasel Sal got the last laugh. His shenanigans did the trick. He delayed the case long enough to throw his client into bankruptcy. My client didn't get a dime. As if I didn't already know it, the practice of law is a game. But the stakes are awfully high and personal.

Seeking a distraction from my day job, I started teaching part-time at a community college. Before the first class, a nervous wave came over me: Who's the tougher audience, a cranky Sal or a roomful of young college students cranking out questions?

In the movie *City Slickers*, Billy Crystal goes on a cattle drive vacation with some buddies, trying to get his smile back. Feeling down about a demotion at work and confused with his place in life, he asks Jack Palance, the wise and irascible cowboy guide named

Curly, what the meaning of life is. Curly holds up a finger, saying just one thing is the secret to life. Excited, Billy asks what it is. To which the sage replies:

"That's what you've got to figure out."

The prior chapters are a crash course in my one thing. In the next section, you'll read about what inspired over a dozen Master Teachers to go into the profession, along with the interesting things they do in class.

PART II

INNOVATIVE MASTER TEACHERS

ADVICE FROM EXPERIENCED INSTRUCTORS AND WHAT INSPIRES THEM

CHAPTER 8

DIANA S. BARBER, J.D.
Lecturer
Robinson College of Business
Georgia State University

What inspired you to teach?

As a young girl of 8 years old, I was encouraged, I mean forced, to accompany my mom to my brother's little league baseball practice at a local high school in Miami, FL. During my endless time of pure boredom, I ventured over to the gymnasium. Outside the gym were metal trash cans and next to them were a stack of unused paper workbooks for a driver's education course. I confiscated them and brought them home with me. The next day, I aligned my favorite stuffed animals, and my brother into my pretend classroom and began teaching them road signs as outlined in the workbooks. Ever since then, I enjoyed teaching and knew that my destiny was to share knowledge with others.

During my time as associate general counsel for a luxury hotel company, I genuinely enjoyed presenting legal concepts and preventative techniques to various departments in the company. When the company passed out our personal copies of "Who Moved My Cheese?" by Dr. Spencer Johnson, I knew it was time for a career change. Teaching hospitality law in a business school felt like a perfect fit. Now, assisting new and transfer students to be professional in a business environment and how to navigate into a successful business career is a blessing and I continue to enjoy teaching.

What teaching methods are most helpful in guiding students toward their goals?

Finding the right teaching methods to assist students in reaching their goals is as individual as motivating employees. Each student has a unique way or ways that work for them. My students get easily distracted when life events happen, such as having to work full-time or take care of a family member, and one of my goals is to keep them on track or assist them in getting back on track. I won't even go into my numerous attempts to compete with social media. Reminding students of "what's in it for me?" helps to reinforce their interest in the material. I attempt to incorporate not only lecturing, but also group work and firsthand experiential learning in the coursework. Actual field trips to businesses are great if they can be arranged. I have found that having weekly checklists for the coursework is really appreciated by students to help keep them on track.

I primarily teach a core business class for freshmen, sophomores, and transfer students to provide a foundation for their business academic career. My large class sizes can be a challenge as it is difficult to get to know all the students on a personal level. In any given semester, I may have 200 students online and another section with 300+ students in a face-to-face hybrid session. The coursework is the same, but the delivery is different. Keeping students engaged is critical whether online or in person. Time spans of attention are short, especially with an online class where students are not made visible to the instructor. Also, jokes are difficult to assess when teaching an online course, but the "LOLs" in the chat do provide inspiration.

One cannot simply lecture the entire class time, or the students will zone out, work on other school subjects, or catch up with their Insta account. I will spend a few minutes at the beginning of each class period discussing one of the majors in our business college and the various student organizations available to students so they can connect with like-minded colleagues. Usually, a representative of the organization or student officer will personally visit the classroom and discuss their experience as a member of a student organization and the value it brings to the students' career objectives. This is done in both types of classes. Then, for the in-person class,

I will usually have the students break out into small groups to have a discussion on a topic along with a visual slide presentation. For the online class, I will ask the students to add to the discussion by speaking or typing in the chat. By the way, it is a good idea to have a graduate student help with monitoring the online class chat during a session, so you don't miss any comments.

Mixing up the delivery methods for both modalities every 15 minutes really helps with engagement in large classes. Lectures, small group discussions, videos, and activities that include standing up in the class (for example, shaking hands when meeting someone and how to best do this necessary networking function), as well as fielding questions and asking others to weigh in on an answer, usually keep students engaged. I typically end both types of classes with what I call Business Etiquette, the unspoken rules in the workplace. Students appreciate the heads up to lessen any future corporate faux pas.

Keeping students engaged is difficult, especially in the large classes I teach. It is not an easy task to individualize the learning, but one tool that helps is having an open-door policy where students can reach out for assistance coupled with my dedication to responding quickly to the needs of students. Being accessible to students is imperative. I use numerous techniques to stay engaged with students, including intelligent agents that will automatically send email messages to students if they miss a quiz or assignment, as a reminder that I am available to assist and that their success is important to me.

What would you like to improve about your teaching?

I would like to improve on the latest techniques for student engagement/success to reach and assist those students who need specialized guidance. Staying abreast of the changing corporate etiquette and protocols requires constant education on my part and insights so I can update my teaching endeavors to stay current and relevant. For example, professional business dress these days does not necessarily require a necktie for gentlemen, except for certain corporate positions. Also, minimal tattoos are now more acceptable in the workforce, yet taboo not too long ago. Understanding Generation Z students will go a long way toward connecting with and reaching these students.

What skills should be emphasized in high school to succeed in your college class?

I would absolutely love to see all high schools offer career development business pathways so students can get a jump on professional dress and other professional skills while gaining assurance that they can do this. Public speaking, although very scary to many, is important to build the confidence needed to be successful. Having student organizations such as Future Business Leaders of America (FBLA) or DECA, Inc. formerly Distributive Education Clubs of America (DECA) in high schools is a great start. I find that those students who were actively involved in student-led business chapters or clubs in high school have a good start in understanding the business world. High schools should also continue to focus on communication, both written and verbal skills, to help students express themselves confidently.

What is the one thing you wished you would have known when you started your teaching career?/Do you have any last bits of wisdom?

Being a successful educator requires endless patience. There are times I am surprised at how uninformed students are to what I consider common sense, which, as we know, is not all that common these days. Basic manners, respect, and the ability to retain and use necessary communication filters do not appear commonplace among students. I would much rather students make mistakes while in college rather than in the workplace. However, decorum used to be taught in the home, and I'm not sure this is a staple or occurring in the homes of some of my students. That is when I step in to provide directions to help students navigate their communication techniques. Patience and a good sense of humor do help. For example, when receiving an email message from a student that began with "Hell, professor," I used this simple typo (the missing "o" on "Hell") to reinforce the necessity for proofreading messages one wants to send to make sure communication is done properly and professionally.

As for a bit of wisdom, I heard an NYU professor recently say that when deciding on a major or career choice, students should not be focused on what they have a passion for but rather on what unique skills they possess. When one focuses only on one's passion, a job in that field may not produce enough income to live the lifestyle they desire. If a unique skill is assimilated and used in finding one's career, the passion will follow as it will provide enough income to sustain a comfortable lifestyle.

CHAPTER 9

JORDAN (JODY) BLANKE, M.S., J.D.
Ernest L. Baskin, Jr. Distinguished Professor of
Computer Science and Law
Stetson-Hatcher School of Business
Mercer University

What inspired you to teach?

I don't believe that there is any one thing that I can point to. During my school years, I always seemed able to explain things well to my fellow classmates. While I was in graduate school, I had an opportunity to be a Teaching Assistant and I enjoyed that a great deal. After practicing law for a few years, I looked into the possibility of teaching a course or two as a part-time instructor. As it happened, St. John's was looking for a full-time instructor and I gave it a shot—no master plan here.

When I look back at teachers I had when I was in school, two names pop out at me. The first was an Earth Science teacher I had at Linden Junior High School in Queens—Harvey Moder. He was a retired fireman and was very dedicated to his students. I happened to have him the year of the Teacher's Strike in New York City. We missed almost two months of school. He invited students to his house during the strike so that we wouldn't get too far behind. He also arranged a trip to a science lab at his alma mater—Hofstra University. It was the first time most of us had been to a college campus. He went out of his way to help us learn.

The second great teacher I had was Robert Greenman at Madison High School in Brooklyn. He taught English and Journalism. He also went way beyond the job description in his teaching and his supervision of the publication of the school newspaper. Back in those days, we had to bring the content to a typesetter to set up the pages for publication. He would drive a few of us to the printing press in Manhattan and we would spend many hours laying out the pages. Mr. Greenman cared greatly about his students. In thinking back on it today, I realize that he understood that each student was different and that he needed to treat each student differently.

What teaching methods are most helpful in guiding students toward their goals?

One thing that I have come to realize is how differently people learn. There is no "One Size Fits All." There are visual learners, auditory learners, kinesthetic learners, and probably other types as well. It becomes particularly challenging because most of my delivery comes by way of four-hour lecture periods. It helps to have PowerPoint presentations for people to read, but it is absolutely necessary to get students engaged in the discussion.

I often begin my law classes with Legal Show and Tell. Students are supposed to bring in stories about legal news that they read, heard, or saw during the past week. For the most part, these are about current events, about which many students have at least some interest. And almost always, I can tie the legal issues to some topic that we will be exploring. It also helps to get as many students as possible involved in the discussion.

I like to teach by example. I think it is much easier to understand an idea if you can see it in action, rather than merely in the abstract. Quite often you can discuss the nuances of the topic by simply varying the facts of the example. Also, I believe that it is imperative to explain why we have certain laws and rules, rather than merely what they are. It is much easier to learn something if you understand the rationale behind it.

Over the last few years, I have had several students come back to visit me and tell me that they miss my stories from class. While I would not have called them stories, I guess some of the examples I use come across to them that way. I'll take it. It appears to work.

And finally, you must not lose sight of the forest for the trees. It is very difficult to learn about something in a vacuum. You must be able to step back and look at the big picture, to understand how and where the law fits in. I try to do this as often as possible in each lecture.

What would you like to improve about your teaching?

One of the biggest challenges I face is to keep the material fresh and entertaining. The last thing I would want someone to say about my class is that it is boring. When I first started teaching, I taught probably 8 or 9 different computer science courses each year. I much preferred that to teaching the same course over and over again. I was continually learning new material and changing my courses because the subject matter changed so rapidly. For the past 25 years or so, I have pretty much been teaching the introductory legal and ethical environment course in our various business degree programs—the BBA, the MBA, the Executive MBA, and the Professional MBA. While each course is somewhat different, the basic topics in law remain very similar. Fortunately, I now teach two different courses in Privacy Law, and I enjoy that there are new developments to learn about and to teach every time I teach the course.

I think it was Joe DiMaggio who, when asked why he always played baseball so hard, responded that someone at the game might be seeing him for their one and only time, and that he wanted to make sure that that person saw him play the game the way it should be played. Before I teach something like contract law, I have to get myself excited about the subject. I have to realize that my students probably don't know much about contract law and that I have to bring energy and enthusiasm to the classroom to make the subject as interesting for them as it is for me.

Online teaching brings many new challenges, including how best to engage students. I use threaded discussions in every class. I find it the most effective way to get students involved, but it is very time-consuming for the instructor. Each time I teach a new section, I tweak some of the parameters, e.g., how many discussions overall, how many days for each discussion, and how many threads. I am still trying to find the best approach.

What skills should be emphasized in high school to succeed in your college class?

As a college professor, I have to emphasize how important it is to be able to write clearly and succinctly. It is extremely important. But I also would like to mention two other skills—probably more accurately described as traits—but traits that can be learned and honed. The first is inquisitiveness. Asking questions is of utmost importance to successful learning. You must ask questions in order to learn—either to yourself or to your teacher. The second is persistence. To truly learn something, you must never give up. If one approach to learning something doesn't work, try another approach. (And by the way, one of the most effective ways to learn something is to teach it. If students in my class have an opportunity to have study groups, I always suggest that they each be responsible for teaching some topics to the others.)

What is the one thing you wished you would have known when you started your teaching career?/Do you have any last bits of wisdom?

Yes. For those high school and college students who do not yet know what they want to major in—don't worry! Take a variety of courses. Take courses that sound interesting to you. Ultimately, you will be most successful in learning about something that interests you or for which you have a passion. Try something different!

CHAPTER 10

YELENA ABALMAZOVA CHAN, ESQ.
Commercial Real Estate and Finance Attorney
Part-Time Instructor
Robinson College of Business
Georgia State University

What inspired you to teach?

For me, it was a selfish reason—I wanted a break in my workweek to do something I truly enjoy. To be clear, I love my lawyer job, but "the grind" can get to you. I have always loved mentoring young attorneys and high school/college students interested in the legal field, so teaching a legal studies class seemed like a great idea to get a bit more fulfillment from my workweek.

What teaching methods are most helpful in guiding students toward their goals?

My approach has been to incorporate real life examples as often as possible for all concepts that I'm trying to solidify in the students. This can be something as simple as sharing an article discussing negligence litigation involving a major corporation and then in the same class showing a clip from *Judge Judy* involving a simple fender bender also based on negligence. In order for the students to fully grasp the concepts, they need to understand the range of how the law can apply. When discussing the products liability material, I bring them a bottle of baby oil and ask them to read the label and tell me why they think this simple household item should be considered a dangerous product. Most of them guess incorrectly (although they are often quite creative in their analysis), but I follow this activity by reading the facts of the Ayers v. Johnson & Johnson Baby Products Co. case discussing how the inhalation of the oil by a baby caused severe permanent injuries because the label lacked a warning.

When we discuss criminal law, we go through a jury selection exercise so they understand the process of how people get picked to be on a jury. I split the class into two groups, one for the prosecution and one for the defense, and ask them to write questions for the potential jurors based on the side of the case they were assigned. This is always quite eye-opening for them, and not surprisingly, as I didn't learn how the process really worked even in law school. When possible, I also like to invite guest speakers to share their real world experiences and insights, particularly for more niche practice areas such as intellectual property and labor law.

What would you like to improve about your teaching?

So much. There is no shortage of things I'd like to improve about my teaching techniques. Just to name a few:

- I always struggle with editing my lectures so that I'm not going too deep into concepts but also making sure I go deep enough for the students to appreciate the complexity of the topic. When I see their eyes start to glaze over, I know I've gone too far.
- Clarity and organization: I can explain an assignment five times in class, but somehow half the class understands it one way and the other half can have a completely different interpretation of the same exact assignment.
- Incorporating technology in beneficial ways into the classroom: So many instructors, including myself, just default to working from the same PowerPoint slides year after year, updating as needed. I want to find a more dynamic method of presenting the materials. The majority of students I've talked to think that slides are a boring way to present information.

- Basing my grading in reality: This is a big struggle because university policies are often not conducive to this approach. In the university setting, if you copy from or consult with your classmates, you are plagiarizing and cheating. In the real lawyer world, if you *don't* consult with your colleagues or use forms previously created by your colleagues, you're committing malpractice. I think it's the college instructor's job to prepare the students for the reality of post-college life, so I'm still developing the best ways to allow students to collaborate on assignments while not running afoul of university policies.

What skills should be emphasized in high school to succeed in your college class?

Where to start?

- Independence: I mean independence on a larger scale, the independence to be personally responsible for your career goals and aspirations. Many students struggle with making decisions about what they want to be when they "grow up." Family, cultural, and societal pressures almost always have a role in this decision. Despite this, I believe everyone should be encouraged to do what they know in their heart is best for them. Students often come to me with a multitude of questions and ask for advice about which career path they should take. My response is always the same: Only YOU know what is best for you. If you don't like accounting, don't be an accountant; if you like rocks, go be a geologist; if you like arguing, don't be a lawyer, that's not what we do. This independence to make a confident decision about one's life path should start way before college. And if you don't have a passion for the classes you're taking because you can't independently make the proper decision about what is best for you, then you won't do well in the class.

- Time Management: I can't describe the number of times I've given students a month to complete an assignment and, without fail, someone comes to me the day that it's due and says they need an extension because [insert excuse du jour here].

- Effective Communication: Effective writing and speaking are crucial skills for success in college and after college. High schools should aim to enhance these core communication skills as a general matter, and while all subjects are important, I believe these two are of superior importance and should be a priority.

What is the one thing you wished you would have known when you started your teaching career?/Do you have any last bits of wisdom?

I wish I knew how differently everyone learns. Effectively teaching something to ten different students may require ten different approaches.

My only advice is to encourage students to explore all careers, classes, and topics that interest them. I really believe it's a duty we have as instructors. I see some students tied to a major just because that's what they chose based on pretty much no research or experience, and they clearly have no passion for it. There is nothing wrong with majoring in accounting but consider interning at a bakery if that's something that piques their interest. Sometimes hearing that from an authority figure like a college professor is encouraging and gives students the permission to explore outside the box.

CHAPTER 11

EVARISTO FERNANDO DORIA, ED.D., M.I.M.
Principal Senior Lecturer
Institute for International Business
Robinson College of Business
Georgia State University

What inspired you to teach?

I have an unwavering passion for sharing knowledge, which has been a constant thread throughout my career. Even before transitioning into a full-time educator, I found myself delivering lectures at prominent universities in the countries where I worked as a senior business executive for a Fortune 100 corporation, driven by a deep desire to impart my expertise and insights to the next generation of leaders.

Furthermore, as I grow older, the notion of leaving a legacy by sharing my knowledge and experience has become an increasingly powerful driver behind my choice to remain an educator. The idea of making a meaningful impact on students' lives and empowering them to achieve their full potential resonates deeply with me.

What teaching methods are most helpful in guiding students toward their goals?

My focus centers on showcasing the tangible applications of their learning, helping them recognize how their knowledge and skills directly correlate with their future aspirations and professional paths.

Moreover, I strongly advocate for active learning, encouraging students to participate in the learning process through various means, such as discussions, problem-solving activities, group work, hands-on projects, and presentations. I encourage you to view the following promotional video showcasing an example of one of the several active learning experiences I've crafted for my students. This particular initiative, titled "Coders for Good" empowers students to create a business plan to drive the digital transformation of towns and small cities while offering affordable living, training, and improved job opportunities for local communities:

www.youtube.com/watch?v=E9E11FHEbQc [1]

Furthermore, I continuously seek out new emerging technology tools to enrich learning experiences, foster interactive learning, and cater to diverse learning styles. In this regard, I would like to highlight a recently developed course that offers a unique approach to understanding business management in Central America. Through the innovative use of virtual reality, students were transported to immersive virtual visits to Panama and Costa Rica, where they practiced the theory learned in the course. For an in-depth look at this initiative, please watch the promotional video available at:

www.youtube.com/watch?v=auVhLmpHlgQ [2]

Finally, I emphasize the importance of cultivating learning ecosystems for enhanced student learning. One example of building a learning ecosystem for my students is the "Meeting Our Exporters" initiative. This ecosystem-based experience fosters an understanding about our exporters and their vital support networks collaborating with prominent institutions and successful export businesses. You're invited to view the promotional video here:

www.youtube.com/watch?v=SAnLnAJfD3s [3]

What would you like to improve about your teaching?

A few months ago, I designed an interdisciplinary learning experience for my international business students that involved fostering collaborative teams across borders comprising both in-

---

1 Dr. Evaristo Doria: Coders for Good. A Unique Learning Experience.
2 Dr. Evaristo Doria: Study Abroad 2021.
3 Dr. Evaristo Doria: Meeting Our Exporters / Minor Int. Business.

ternational business and engineering students. You can view the promotional video for this learning experience here:

www.youtube.com/watch?v=m_RGHFtX9F0 [4]

As I look ahead, I am enthusiastic about expanding my efforts to create more cross-border interdisciplinary learning experiences. Such experiences not only prompt participants to critically analyze novel ideas and challenges but also encourage them to delve into the intricate intersections of various fields of study while developing their global mindset. Overall, I believe that interdisciplinary teaching is essential for shaping future leaders in business.

What skills should be emphasized in high school to succeed in your college class?

Continuing to prioritize the education of high school students in STEM, applied creativity, and ethics is very important. Within the realm of STEM education, it is imperative to cultivate students' curiosity regarding emerging technologies and their potential applications. It's unfortunate that formal education sometimes hampers creativity rather than fostering it. This underscores the urgency for high school educators to consistently nurture applied creativity in their students. As routine tasks become more automated by intelligent machines, the ability to innovate becomes essential. Finally, I firmly advocate for the continued emphasis on teaching ethics to high school students. This endeavor not only equips them with the skills to foster prosperous enterprises but also contributes to the betterment of society at large.

What is the one thing you wished you would have known when you started your teaching career?/Do you have any last bits of wisdom?

I am strongly convinced of the importance of establishing environments within educational institutions that encourage educa-

---

[4] Dr. Evaristo Doria: University of Toronto/Good Business Initiative.

tors to experiment with new technologies, ultimately leading to the creation of enhanced learning experiences. However, it's crucial to remember that while technology is important, the human touch in education remains extremely vital. In this regard, I had the privilege of co-presenting at a web conference titled "Emotional Design Thinking in IB Education." This event was supported by the GSU Center for International Business Education and Research (CIBER) and the recording is available online.

You can view the promotional video for this conference through this link:

www.youtube.com/watch?v=3Y5ZAaplDuI [5]

---

[5] Dr. Evaristo Doria: Emotional Design Thinking in IB Education.

CHAPTER 12

L. GREGORY (GREG) HENLEY, MBA, PH.D.
Entrepreneur and Filmmaker
Former Director, Center for Entrepreneurship
Robinson College of Business
Georgia State University

What inspired you to teach?

During my business career, I noticed that a lot of people, especially people of color, have started businesses. However, many of the same people seemed to have trouble running the businesses effectively. I thought that I could help people (of all colors) run businesses more effectively, so I went back to school with that objective in mind. Since my Ph.D. program, I taught entrepreneurship and business strategy at business schools and, hopefully, my students can run a business better than if they hadn't taken my class.

What teaching methods are most helpful in guiding students toward their goals?

In the classroom, I try to relate everything back to the real world so students can relate to something they are familiar with. This includes bringing in businessmen, using case studies, and talking about some of my business experiences. In addition, whenever possible, I like students to reach out to the business community. Examples of this include assignments for students to interview entrepreneurs and internships. For business classes, application of the material is critical to prepare students for the real world. So, telling them something and asking them to take a multiple choice question may be good for some things, but is a poor method for many business concepts. Getting the students to apply what they've learned is a goal. Often, this can be done via case studies and sometimes by working on projects for businesses. Some of the more challenging (for me and the students), but rewarding courses I've taught involved students working for real businesses. The students are able to apply business concepts and see how businesses are actually run—the good, the bad, and especially the ugly.

What would you like to improve about your teaching?

It's very important that I reach the students on their level. If I can get their attention, then I can teach them. Improving my teaching requires that I get constructive feedback to ensure that what I'm doing is working. As I get older, using tools that are consistent with the way students learn can become more challenging, so I need to work to make sure that I'm communicating in ways they grasp. So what I'd like to improve is my knowledge and understanding of what is important to our students.

What skills should be emphasized in high school to succeed in your college class?

The skills that should be emphasized are certainly business skills. But, more broadly, I'd like for students to be able to think more analytically and in more depth. Other specific skills are a basic grasp of math and, importantly, writing skills.

What is the one thing you wished you would have known when you started your teaching career?/Do you have any last bits of wisdom?

The value of testing early whether the students understand the material I'm presenting. In one of my first classes, I presented the material and got the verbal feedback I hoped for when I asked questions that indicated the students understood what I was telling them. However, when it came to applying the material for an assignment, the students did poorly—and my hopes and expectations were dashed. What I learned is that some of the early exercises, questions, and tests that I needed to implement should be better tied to what I expected the students to learn. Also, that I needed to implement those exercises, questions, and tests earlier in the semester so that I have time to make adjustments if I need to. The other thing I learned is that quite a few students are in the class to get a grade, but not necessarily to learn. This is in contrast to me whose primary reason for being in the classroom is because I want to teach.

CHAPTER 13

LEILA LAWLOR, J.D., M.B.A., M.S., M.A.
Director of Academic Excellence Program and
Professor of Practice
Washington and Lee University School of Law

What inspired you to teach?

I love school, and I always have. People thrive in jobs which they enjoy and about which they are passionate. I am passionate about teaching, and I thoroughly enjoy both sides of the educational process; thus, I am good at school—simply because I enjoy it so much.

I was raised by two educators who taught me that education is an honor and a gift. My father was a college journalism professor back when newspapers (with emphasis on the paper part of the word) were delivered to our door each morning. He trained students who left his classes ready to produce grammatical, concise, interesting news articles. His students used to joke that my father spent more time marking their papers with his red pen than they had spent writing their papers. My father took his responsibility as an educator very seriously because he realized the capacity of education to change lives. His own education had provided him with opportunities that his parents had certainly not enjoyed. My father taught me that making the most of one's education can open many doors. He also taught me that, for an educator, building mentoring relationships with students is essential to enjoying the process of teaching. For students, these relationships can prove key when they are later looking for career advice or for a recommendation for employment or graduate school.

My mother taught English grammar, English and American literature, and journalism at the high school level. She had a gift for engaging her students. For their instruction and enjoyment, my mother would read classic literature to her students in the late afternoons, when they would otherwise have been tired and eager for the bell to ring. My mother was a wonderful reader and raconteur. As she read to her students, her animated voice changed when she switched between characters' voices. When a character in the book she was reading was unhappy, my mother's face and voice would convey that emotion. Her students were mesmerized. My mother would pause periodically to invite spirited discussion of the predicaments in which the literary characters had found themselves. I attended a public elementary school across the street from the high school where my mother taught. The elementary school day ended earlier than the high school, so each afternoon I would walk across the street and quietly join my mother's classroom to hear her regale her students with *The Scarlet Letter, The Old Man and the Sea,* or *Romeo and Juliet.* My mother taught me that effective teaching means making the process enjoyable. She taught me that lazy, unprepared teaching was unacceptable. She also taught me to care deeply about the process and about each student.

What teaching methods are most helpful in guiding students toward their goals?

One important rule is that teachers should not spoon feed. It is much more effective to draw students to a conclusion by leading them through critical analysis in an interactive format rather than to deliver information by unilateral lecture. If students are engaged in analytical thinking during lively classroom interaction, they are much more likely to draw accurate conclusions, remember both the learning process and the conclusions, and retain the material long-term. My mother's philosophy: mediocre teachers lecture; master teachers conduct interactive classrooms.

In the same vein of thought, teachers should do their absolute best to make their classrooms engaging. Humor is a wonderful addition to any classroom, but not all teachers are gifted comedians.

If humor is not your strong point, just remember not to take yourself too seriously. Even a brilliant professor in a structured and challenging undergraduate or graduate school classroom should be approachable.

If you have chosen to teach, you have chosen to place students at the center of your professional universe. Tell them. They will appreciate knowing how much you want them to thrive, to enjoy your teaching, and to meet their academic and professional goals. As you get to know your students, they will surely appreciate your interest in their lives and goals.

Praise your students' efforts when they are worthy of praise, and help students visualize the timeline for obtaining their goals. Your words will help minimize attrition, as you will be validating your students' efforts and helping them realize the tasks ahead are surmountable. For example, if they are finishing up their first semester of college, congratulate them on making it one-eighth of the way through college. If they are finishing their second year, congratulate them on completing half of a college degree. Encourage them to pause and reflect on their accomplishments and the rigors and complexities of the studies they have completed.

Encourage students to create a systematized schedule which includes unmovable obligations, as well as time for recreation and self-care. Many college students must balance work and family obligations along with school, so systematized scheduling is essential. Students who are unsuccessful in completing their academic goals often have gotten waylaid by the unexpected demands of other obligations. When things start to become unmanageable in one of the other spheres our students are balancing, their academic workload can simultaneously seem to snowball out of control. Without a systematized schedule, a student in this predicament may soon miss multiple assignments and start to feel that it would be impossible to catch up with the rest of the class.

An added benefit to developing relationships and building community among your students is that your students will feel they have someone with whom to communicate if they have an issue arise that is negatively impacting their ability to study. If students perceive you as a caring and approachable professor, they will undoubtedly feel more comfortable reaching out to you for help.

If you have built a community among your students, they will also have classmates on whom they can lean. If your community-building efforts prove effective in retaining students who would otherwise falter, you are playing a pivotal role in enabling student success. Additionally, the relationships your students build with classmates might prove to be the start of their forming a professional network.

What would you like to improve about your teaching?

I know that energy-infused teaching is the best kind of teaching, but sometimes other responsibilities, routine tasks, and worries can drain me of the energy and enthusiasm that I want to give each of my students. This is especially true when I teach three-hour class sessions that end in the evening. Ironically, I think the cure for my shortage of evening energy is the same thing I advise students to do—reserve energy by maintaining a careful schedule while carving out pockets of time for rest. And I have learned from my students, of course, the magical power of an occasional energy drink.

What skills should be emphasized in high school to succeed in your college class?

There are numerous skills necessary for success in college—determination, team building, self-discipline, perseverance, and the ability to write succinctly and effectively. Time management is a learned skill, and the students who start college best prepared are usually those who were involved in high school extracurriculars or outside employment, while also taking rigorous classes. Even when students come to college lacking time management skills, they can succeed if they buckle down and take the advice of university study-skills experts; but the best chances for success exist when students have developed the art of time management while still in high school.

Another important and often overlooked skill that is necessary for success in higher education is the ability to deal with stress. Interestingly, the American Bar Association now mandates training on wellness practices. In its oversight of accredited U.S. law schools, the ABA has recently amended one of its governing standards, Standard 303, which the ABA now interprets to require "development of professional identity [which] should involve an intentional exploration of the values, guiding principles, and well-being practices considered foundational to successful legal practice." In other words, not only does the ABA recognize that law school is stressful, the ABA also now expects its accredited law schools to train students in wellness practices. I preach to my students that they must reserve time for exercise, for recreation, and for enjoying the people they love. They must schedule time for these things. They must also carve out tiny bits of time to enjoy the world around them without the ubiquitous electronic distractions of our modern world. For example, they might pause to enjoy their first cup of coffee in the morning, truly tasting its robust flavor and smelling its heady aroma—if possible, while listening to birds in the yard around them—but not while checking texts or reading the morning's headlines on their phones.

Mindfulness techniques need not be time consuming, and they can make a tremendous difference in managing the stress of a busy college student's life. Sometimes all it takes is being especially aware of one's pleasant surroundings, being present in the moment rather than focused on the next task or the day ahead. A mindfulness instructor who recently visited one of my classes taught me to clear my head for a few moments during my short walk from the parking lot to the law school building. Even in the major metropolis where I have taught for the past fifteen years, I can hear birds and feel the wind on my face. This mindfulness technique provides me with a sense of ready as I enter the building to begin my workday.

What is the one thing you wish you would have known when you started your teaching career?/Do you have any last bits of wisdom?

Yes, absolutely! My own teaching mentor is Professor L. Lynn Hogue, a wonderful, brilliant man who taught me Constitutional Law in the 1990s. He was a superb law professor. He loved the process, and that was obvious to all students lucky enough to enroll in his classes. I can still remember him teaching my class *Marbury v. Madison*, the landmark Supreme Court case that established the Court's authority and duty to perform judicial review. This case was the foundation for all the other cases we would discuss for two semesters. It was grand knowledge! His class was honestly more enjoyable than eating chocolate. The material we covered in his classes was complex and challenging, but his inspired teaching has enabled my retention of the material for decades. When I first started teaching in 2008, Lynn Hogue and I met for lunch, and I gushed telling him how much I was enjoying teaching. I told him how lucky I felt to be able to teach college classes. His response: "We are not just lucky, Leila; we are blessed." If you are reading this chapter because you are new to college teaching, please realize what an honor you have been bestowed. Make the most of it. Pour your heart into it. Make a difference to the students you are privileged to teach. Get to know their names, their dreams, and their challenges, and you will be blessed too.

CHAPTER 14

LAURA E. MEYERS, PH.D.
Artist Scholar
Clinical Professor
Program Coordinator, Master of Arts
in Creative & Innovative Education Program
Georgia State University

What inspired you to teach?

When I was in undergrad, I couldn't decide on a major. I tried art, Spanish, business, theatre, accounting, English, sociology, psychology, etc. I remember bumping into one of my professors in the stairwell on the way to class. He knew I hadn't committed yet but needed to, and he casually suggested elementary education. I should have known to start there. It included an array of subject areas plus art, music, P.E., and more. It was an all-in-one opportunity.

My mom taught middle school English, and I adored helping in her classroom. Decorating bulletin boards, grading papers, rearranging desks, reading the novels she taught. Younger me thought all of the behind-the-scenes work was so cool. My grandfather also taught—I now have the school bell he used to ring sitting on my desk. Older me loves this reminder of the educators in my family.

What inspires me to continue teaching is my love of learning, creating, and storytelling. I see curriculum all around me. I'm constantly pondering if something I'm reading might fit into a class I'm teaching or if my college students might enjoy learning this week through painting abstract portraits or deconstructing a script I wrote. I look forward to uncovering what students noticed in our texts—especially personal and professional connections—and how they might apply what we're studying in their own teaching and learning spaces with young learners.

Teaching is mentoring. I enjoy listening, asking questions, and providing support so students develop their own agency within academic, professional, and personal contexts.

Students, especially graduate students, follow up with me after graduation and fill me in on their accomplishments. Teacher of the Year awards, new jobs, advocacy efforts, doctoral program pursuits, relationships and children, entrepreneurial endeavors, publications of articles and picture books, leadership roles—the list goes on! My students inspire me.

What teaching methods are most helpful in guiding students toward their goals?

Build community. When students feel connections to others in the learning space, they're more likely to participate in discussions and activities. For some students, contributing can feel intimidating, but I don't want to miss out on learning from my students and the innate genius they bring into our learning space. Community can be cultivated in several ways and in a short amount of time. The key is consistency. Before the start of each class, I greet students as they enter our space whether it's in-person or synchronous online. Interestingly, students tend to follow suit even in our virtual spaces by tossing a note into our chat, posting an emoji, or unmuting to say hello.

The majority of my class sessions are 2.5–3 hours. When our session starts, I dedicate the first 5-15 minutes (it varies) for a community building activity. I pose a question or provide a prompt and invite students to share their responses with a partner or small group. (breakout rooms if virtual) I've collected a lot of prompts over the years, but I can share three popular ones that I use pretty regularly across all courses.

Share a rose (something beautiful/exciting happening in your world), rosebud (something you're looking forward to or something in process—about to bloom), *or* thorn. (something you're powering through or a prickly situation that happened recently) A rose might include eating out at a new restaurant while a rosebud could be looking forward to starting a new job. Thorns vary from not getting enough sleep to the loss of a loved one.

Choose an emoji that best shows how you're doing in this moment. If meeting online, I ask students to drop an emoji into our chat. Students seem to really like this one and typically share more than one emoji along with a story to match. Sometimes, I'll ask for an emoji at the end of class to describe how they're feeling about new content discussed during class.

I also enjoy posting 3–5 photos that center on a specific topic and asking students which one best reflects something about them and why. Some collections of photos that have been received well by students include: (1) characters from popular streaming shows; (2) nature/outdoor scenes; and (3) theme-decorated cupcakes.

After students chat with their partner or small group, I always share my own response with the whole group. It's my hope that if students see me sharing, they'll take a risk too. Then, I ask if a couple of people want to share with the class too. We usually have 3-4 volunteers offer up brief responses.

Here's the thing—because we make a little time to connect, students shift into being more present and participatory in class activities and assignments. Discussions are reflective, insightful, and beneficial. All students are willing to participate. (or they don't mind me as much when nudging them to participate)

Because my class sessions are very discussion-based, I'm constantly trying new strategies. I absolutely love-love using "critical friends protocols"* that the National School Reform Faculty provides free for anyone to use. One of my favorites is the Four-A Text Protocol which asks students: What *assumptions* does the author of the text have? What do you *agree* with in the text? What do you

---

* nsrfharmony.org/protocols/

want to *argue* with in the text? What ideas in the text do you want to *aspire* to? Students begin by sharing assumptions but dive deep into conversation and organically address the other questions. At the end, I need to know how they'll apply what they've learned in their own classroom or other learning spaces: What does this mean for our work with young learners?

What would you like to improve about your teaching?

My area of study is education—mainly creative and innovative education and elementary education—so I'm constantly reflecting on improving my teaching when developing each course and even each class session. I coach in-service and pre-service educators in becoming reflective practitioners, so it is especially important that I "practice what I preach": *What went well? What might need to be altered? How do I know?* I'm not only scaffolding students' understanding and exploration of theory to practice with frameworks and methodologies. Ultimately, I'm cultivating students' pedagogical identities as culturally responsive, justice-oriented educators.

Improving the systems my students are navigating—that's a needed shift. My hope is that my students find and maintain joy in the work they're pursuing—and—I recognize the challenges presented within a career in the field of education. Racial injustices, school shootings, suicides, global pandemic. Plus, the state of Georgia passed HB-1084, which purports that racism and bias are "divisive concepts." Additionally, this bill is harmful to our transgender youth—a demographic that needs our protection.

Over the years, I've also broadened what counts as texts for courses. For me, texts can be anything that a student reads, views, or listens to in preparation for class including but not limited to journal articles, book chapters, TED Talks, podcasts, interviews, short films, documentaries, picture books, music/song lyrics, news stories, novels, and even pieces of art. And, in addition to inviting students to seek and use texts that connect to our topics (student choice is important), I make every effort to assign texts by an array of creators. I'm very fortunate that the demographics of our student body at my university has such a diverse representation of backgrounds—race, language, culture, first-generation, religion, sexuality, ability, age, work-life experience, etc.

What and how we study in any of my class sessions needs to reflect and expand the complex, intersectional identities of my students.

What skills should be emphasized in high school to succeed in your college class?

First, kudos to our high school educators. We owe them a huge thanks and a standing ovation for sharing their expertise and supporting young people with learning *and "how to life."*

Continue cultivating curiosity. Curious college students want to read, ask questions, share ideas, listen to others, record notes, seek clarity, pursue various perspectives, take risks, sketch designs, innovate, problem-solve, make mistakes, imagine, gather collaborators, create, and more. To me, curiosity requires vulnerability, and vulnerability requires courage.

Creating and maintaining safe spaces to *practice curiosity* across content areas and contexts encourages high school students to ask, "What if? Why not?" Those questions are excellent starting points for so many class discussions and assignments. What if we tried...? Why not dig deeper into...?

What is the one thing you wished you would have known when you started your teaching career?/Do you have any last bits of wisdom?

Unlearn. We need to deconstruct what we know and consider how we learned this and who it favors. Unlearning is one way to reduce bias and, in turn, harm. Unlearning can lead to allyship (and more) which is beneficial to our students (and us) in "becoming" educators. Aren't we always growing and becoming?

Give yourself and your students grace. We're human. Educators make mistakes. Students make mistakes. Assume positive intent and ask your students to do the same with you and keep it moving.

Protect your well-being. It's so much harder to support your students, colleagues, family members, etc. when you aren't your best self. Make time to rest. Set boundaries.

Please know that I'm saying all of this aloud to myself too. We have one precious life. *One*. Figure out what you want out of it, what you want to put into it, who you want on this journey with you—all the things. Then, make it count.

CHAPTER 15

ISABELLE N. MONLOUIS, MBA, DBA
Professor of Practice
Associate Director, Russell Center for Entrepreneurship
Georgia State University

What inspired you to teach?

I didn't want to teach. In many ways, this was the "family business." As a willful high school graduate, I craved travel, adventure, and making my own way instead. So, I traveled from Europe to America and pursued careers in risk management and global innovation consulting. Each career change required upskilling, and I fell in love with learning and the many possibilities that it opened. Teaching became a priority when I became a manager. I remembered all the transformational teachers, professors, and corporate trainers who helped me grow, and I knew that it was time to pay it forward.

As a newly minted MBA, I joined a company famous for its immunity to change—the one started by Hamilton. As employees, we used to joke that Hamilton left for his renowned duel saying, "Don't touch anything until I come back." And that they are still waiting. Except that I had a staff of employees to upskill for the emerging work of the Risk department and no vehicle to train them. I left that bank for a global company known to train its employees so well that the entire industry would pay a premium to hire from there rather than train their own personnel. Yet, even there, innovating meant that the training department had not yet caught up to our needs.

I remember the terrifying moment when I realized I did not know what to do until I understood that no one else did either. How different from the case studies with scripted answers of my academic days? My dual MBA/MA in Economics had given me a strong foundation in mixed methods, and somehow, we found insights, codified our approaches, modified strategies, and the work became more manageable. I became a corporate master trainer to support the upskilling and reskilling of my colleagues nationally and internationally. Then I extended this work to preferred customers and suppliers across multiple industries until I elected to focus on supporting corporate innovation teams.

After completing my doctorate a decade ago, I decided to teach at the university because I believe that entrepreneurship and innovation, problem-solving, tech, and data literacy are skills that every graduate needs to master to successfully navigate the level of disruption permeating our current business environment. That this third career is proving to be more stimulating than I ever anticipated makes me chuckle whenever I remember my initial reservations.

What teaching methods are most helpful in guiding students toward their goals?

Giving my students a reason to show up, engage fully, and quickly apply what they have learned is most effective. Fortunately, entrepreneurship is a topic that captures their imagination long before they fall in love with their own business idea. I often set the stage for a new topic with a "ripped from the headlines" section at the beginning of the class. Facebook losing $232 billion in value overnight or the ongoing saga of the leadership of X—the company formerly known as Twitter—provide live case studies of the importance of understanding business models. Social media's impact in amplifying controversies brings NIL deal valuations to a more relatable level. I am deliberate in using the news to extend beyond the formal learning experience of the classroom to encompass every media impression related to that company. I query the students to find out who heard about the headline. From "What happened," ... more students chime in with the "What does it mean?" and we usually end with "Why it matters" as a transition to our weekly class topic. First, they pay attention in case it comes up in class again, and it usually does, as I thread the example throughout the semester. Hopefully, by the end of the semester, they will have become more accustomed to thinking from the leadership chair of the businesses they love to patronize and have become more entrepreneurially literate.

I often ask them to choose the topics or the companies we study—or note their areas of interest during introductions. As often as possible, students will select industries, companies, or products they care about. And we will develop these exemplars together. Or they will work on developing their own ventures. In this way, the work remains relevant and exciting to them, and they essentially co-design the class. It's a mixed blessing to hear students report, "I actually feel like I learned something in this class." Or that it was worthwhile. Or "This is the one class I looked forward to attending." One of my favorite classes is designed so they can go from persistent problems to vetted prototypes and use their class artifacts as applications to university entrepreneurship competitions. Students love this class. Many have won hundreds of thousands of dollars in national entrepreneurship grants and competitions, and a few are currently talking to VCs in Silicon Valley. I call it the class that pays you back in cash, connections, and street cred.

What would you like to improve about your teaching?

Emerging research shows that fields like entrepreneurship and innovation attract a more significant proportion of neuroatypical people. That is certainly consistent with my observations in class. While neuroatypical—or neurospicy as they sometimes prefer to be called to tone down the stigma—have brains that thrive on innovation, their strengths are less suited to the rigidity of a traditional classroom. For example, a student becomes an A+ student and maintains an A+ average by zealously following all the rules. To preserve their hard-won A+, they follow rules and rubrics, a clearly defined path to success, and expect certainty that they will achieve a perfect score. And God helps the faculty member who fails to deliver on that safe A+ expectation. A mere A will trigger an identity crisis of Shakespearian proportions. These students are hardworking and very disciplined. They have high academic grit and a low tolerance for risk or ambiguity.

In contrast, most students with entrepreneurial grit thrive on ambiguity and delight in breaking and remaking the rules—these were just suggestions, right? These skills generate market success, but classroom experiences often brand them as having less potential. They are rarely A students, and they don't care. We're lucky to keep them interested beyond the launch of their business, especially if they do not find the curriculum useful and immediately relevant.

I look forward to developing teaching tools and methods that are more neurospicy-friendly. I realized I was on the right track when a class erupted in spontaneous applause after introducing a 2-page visual syllabus as an alternative to the 12+ pages of dense text my colleagues and I used. After all, am I testing their ability to read the syllabus—which might be challenging for a student with dyslexia—or their ability to innovate a product idea or validate a business model?

What skills should be emphasized in high school to succeed in your college class?

Students need to learn how to fail forward. Learning to fail and learning from failure, with no loss of enthusiasm. Trying again, knowing this time, you are trying with the benefit of experience so you will be more successful.

We have much to unlearn. Students need to unlearn playing it safe enough to avoid failure. And we need to learn how to teach without penalizing "failure" but instead recontextualizing it as gathering valuable information to make their next attempt more successful.

What is the one thing you wished you would have known when you started your teaching career?/Do you have any last bits of wisdom?

I wish I had known to teach less so they could learn more. It means choosing fewer main instruction topics and minimizing lecture time in favor of more hands-on application. This matters because sometimes the student who struggles most is the student who works hardest while juggling tremendous responsibilities. Always err on the side of empathy.

CHAPTER 16

BENITA HARRIS MOORE, PH.D.
Professor Emeritus
Clayton State University and
Retired Curriculum Program Specialist
Technical College System of Georgia

What inspired you to teach?

Unlike many young people, I did not always aspire to become a teacher. I was not opposed to teaching, but it just did not seem that was the direction I would go. I began my college career as an undeclared major but thought the science field was where I might end up. I began working at a local small loan company and found I really enjoyed bookkeeping, administrative work, business, and helping people. I then changed my major to Secretarial Studies (as it was known at that time), and I thoroughly enjoyed the courses. Toward the end of my associate degree, I realized I did not want to just do this kind of work all day but wanted to help others develop and learn the skills needed to be successful in a business and office environment. Thus my major became business education at my four-year college. I continued to work in offices for a good many years part-time during college and even full-time during the summer and on breaks. Selecting business education as a major and education as a career was a great decision for me, and I believe I was able to help many students as they navigated their education and began their careers.

What teaching methods are most helpful in guiding students toward their goals?

I found that getting students involved in their education was a key to guiding students toward their goal. I did hands-on learning with students before it became popular. Many of the students I taught learned better by doing than just reading or by a lecture, so I adapted my teaching style to fit the needs of my students. Of course, every class was different, but I always paid attention to how students responded to the material I was teaching. I also found that being flexible was a benefit. Sometimes I would have a great presentation prepared (at least I thought it was great), but I could tell students were not grasping the subject ... so I would take a different approach to cover the material. Having students invested in their own learning is important for student success.

What would you like to improve about your teaching?

As long as I was teaching, I was always looking for new ideas and creative ways to present information to students. I always felt I could improve and continued to learn. In my field, business education, you had to continue to learn, and technology played a huge role in my continuing to learn and continuing to improve. In the mid-1990's, my college became the second public "laptop university" in the nation, where every student was required to have the same computer. This meant that I had to adjust my teaching style to accommodate the technology being used. Students were paying for computers and expected teachers to use them to enhance the learning process. Since all students had laptops, I eventually "flipped" my classroom and had students doing different types of assignments outside of class than were previously used. My in-class time also looked different.

I am now retired, but I continue to be interested in and fascinated by how technology is used in the classroom as well as new teaching methods. I can only imagine how AI would impact the development of my presentations ... and I am sure something else will be along after AI and after the next "new" technology.

What skills should be emphasized in high school to succeed in your college class?

I believe business, technology, and life skills need to be gained while in high school as well as writing and analytical skills. A student who can think and process and write should be able to be successful in college and life. A student with an understanding of business, technology, and life skills should be able to succeed in college and life also.

What is the one thing you wished you would have known when you started your teaching career?/Do you have any last bits of wisdom?

When I began teaching, I was determined to share ALL of my knowledge with my students. While sharing and teaching knowledge is important, I quickly learned that being interested in the student was equally important. Fortunately, I had some good mentors who made me realize that Theodore Roosevelt had it right years before I began teaching: "Nobody cares how much you know until they know how much you care." I can't stress how important it is to know a little (or a lot) about your students. Knowing this information will positively impact your effectiveness and influence in the classroom.

Something else I wished I was told before I began teaching was that being open to opportunities was okay. I realized that it was okay to be open to different paths and opportunities; but before I figured it out, I struggled with that decision. What I would tell a new teacher is flexibility is key. No two students or two classes are the same, so being flexible is key. In addition, if you are offered a new responsibility that is not "pure teaching," be open to it. The new opportunity may or may not take you from the classroom but may open doors that are different than you could have imagined. Don't be afraid to accept these opportunities. My 40+ years in education was enhanced because I said "yes" to opportunities that were presented to me, even if the new challenge was outside of my comfort zone. If I had not said yes to some of the opportunities, I may not have been happy in my field for 40+ years, so as I said before ... being open to opportunities and being flexible is important.

CHAPTER 17

CAROL SPRINGER SARGENT, CPA, PH.D.
Associate Professor of Accounting
Stetson-Hatcher School of Business
Mercer University

What inspired you to teach?

As a young girl I loved learning. I would get excited about what I learned and wanted to share it with others. Sharing it made it even more fun and motivating, sparking more learning. It was not until later in life that I came to appreciate that learning was not just fun but empowering and life-changing. Learning changes the trajectory of one's life, both in terms of financial stability, access to interesting problems, and overall personal well-being. This sparked my "mentor" chapter, working with young professionals in the corporate world. As my career grew, I authored training for finance teams and that spawned the "what about curriculum" chapter. Curriculum design was the final straw to toggle me from corporate to academia where I try to build financially competent professionals with fewer tears and more successful outcomes.

What teaching methods are most helpful in guiding students toward their goals?

This is a tricky question because each learner brings a unique constellation of tendencies, frustrations, academic backgrounds, and goals. "Most helpful" is specific to the learner. For me, the best way to help a student achieve their goals is to coach them and curate their learning strategy, generally one-on-one in office hours or after class. I do some of this during class, generally after the first test, since low scores tend to lead to a discussion on learning strategies. We learn a little brain science. What improves memory for content, especially content you do not find interesting? What are best/worst practices of learners? We analyze assessments, which I give weekly. Did you mostly miss theory or computations? What might you do to adjust based on that pattern? Then I invite them for a personal consultation to explore their learning fingerprint. We run experiments. Read the chapter for one unit. Did that help? Watch my YouTube videos for a different chapter, did that help? We get very creative at times, including setting timers, drawing pictures, changing locations or device settings, and always with humor and genuine care for them as individuals. Once you help them maximize their learning style, it applies to other classes too!

My suggestions are often simple and classic. (though they can get bizarre on occasion) I once had a failing student agree to do all the assigned homework as an experiment. As you might guess, it went quite well. He came back at the end of the semester to see me with a big grin. He started to make high grades in his other classes by doing the homework. We both had a good laugh. This semester, a star pitcher on the baseball team came to see me with failing scores. He has test anxiety. How do you handle batters with performance anxiety? "That's different," he says. Well, what about imagining each question as a batter? He was stunned. I made a new friend and his next exam grade was 89. Talking about learning opens the door for students to share with me what is not working so we can craft an experiment and get to success. This collaboration creates a bond and reframes my role to coach, especially for those that come see me one-on-one. Does this take time? Yes. Is it my job to teach them to learn *and* think? That is not a fight that interests me. Helping students to learn is immensely rewarding and makes the accounting medicine go down more smoothly.

My most popular technique to this day was the result of a learning experiment with a struggling student. He just hated the accounting. I asked him if he would just give me the commercial breaks during Law and Order. (his favorite show) He agreed. I created three-minute coaching videos that taught a core idea in each video. I focused on one foundational idea that, if missed, would make the rest of the chapter impossible. The "just three minutes" was a wild success. Students can handle three minutes of accounting. It turns out you can learn a ton in three minutes of *undivided attention*. The other thing I noticed about these videos is that they ensure the prerequisites are in place for later chapters. If a student gets stuck later because they did not know an earlier concept, they get a three-minute video prescription. To this day, 14 years after the first video, these are mentioned on my student evaluations more than any other topic. Sadly, it took a lot of time to boil down chapters into what is *essential*. (I thought it was all essential!) I learned to sequence the material better and make the core ideas my centerpiece.

Of course, there are best practices for classroom management and curriculum design. I like to orchestrate my lessons from easy to complex and connect them to prior lessons and lessons across the curriculum, if possible. This requires me to learn what is going on across the curriculum, outside my area. It helps students to know how they will recycle this less-than-lovely (to them at least) accounting concept in their major courses and in their careers. I also stay flexible and adapt to my class. I once had an introductory accounting class with 90% healthcare majors. We shifted to learning about healthcare accounting and the class climate and motivation improved remarkably.

What would you like to improve about your teaching?

I adopt a high demand high support teaching philosophy. I expect a lot and so I get some student grousing. I wish I had creative ways to help them see that their effort, considerable from their view, pays off later. I teach complex material, often tainted with math phobia, that many find boring. I wonder about how to motivate them to expend effort. I try new things. I would like to improve how I frame my expectations in a convincing way. I want to put lipstick on the accounting pig!

I struggle with wanting to teach more topics and more techniques. I have learned that when I teach, it does not mean *they learned*. So, I need to constantly assess the learning. With countless learning experiments, evolving curricula, fancy websites, and glitzy technologies, all of which I love and use, I still have not found the accelerate button on brain chemistry! But I continue to try ways to make learning more efficient (fewer tries to mastery) and more effective. (longer memory and ability to transfer to new tasks)

What skills should be emphasized in high school to succeed in your college class?

At a basic level, I would encourage, where possible, go deep into at least one topic in the subject, preferably something of the student's choice. Debate it. Thinking about the important questions of that topic. Do authentic work around this topic. Then write about it, since writing requires both comprehension and communication skills. Avoid skipping across the surface, requiring only remembering and a steady diet of multiple-choice tests. When you get deep, you find the interesting questions requiring critical thinking. It becomes a model for learning and moving up the hierarchy from remembering to thinking. Thinking and transferring what you know to other problems will span a career.

A dose of financial literacy and basic numeracy skills will serve them for a lifetime. It will also help in accounting. Maybe spend a little less time on special triangles and the quadratic equation. Instead, solve for "x" and work with fractions, especially in a word problem where they must create the formula from the situation. Yes, they learned it in sixth grade. *They forgot it.* Use practical consumer-based problems so they see the relevance. For instance, solve for price per unit, interest rate, or ending balance on the account after activity.

What is the one thing you wished you would have known when you started your teaching career?/Do you have any last bits of wisdom?

Setting expectations matter. Take time to craft a short thoughtful syllabus. Give them lots of chances to learn. (formative assessments) Give them a clear target. I give a list of all the questions on the major exams. Not the actual questions. But a list. Question 1 is on depreciation. Question 2 is on bad debts. This reduces uncertainty. There *will be* a question on XXX on the exam. It increases the chances they will study that thing. It means I have to craft exams that are comprehensive. (because otherwise they ignore what is not on it) I can live with that.

The expression that "they do not care what you know until they know you care." It applies. You show that you care in simple ways. Learn their names. Show up on time, with an interesting plan. Be enthusiastic. Be responsive. I give out my cell phone. I answer texts and emails immediately. Most of these inquiries stem from something in the student's world that is disrupting their academic plan and we talk about that. However, if I get a bunch about an assignment, I whip up another three-minute video and it settles down. I missed an "essential skill."

I ask on the syllabus to care more about the learning than the grade. The grade is fleeting; exercising the brain builds neurons and habits. Grades matter as a form of feedback. I accept that we need to report the learning outcomes. (grades) A student that attends and adjusts their learning practices will be a "point magnet." Those on a hunting mission for points may or may not learn.

Never lose their trust. I want them to *think* so I try to walk that fine line between what I want them to do without doing it for them. For many, problems without correct answers terrify them. It gets better over time if trust is in place. If you say XXX is on the test, do not change your mind. I change dates on practice assignments (like homework) if a student respectfully asks. I can count on one hand the number of times a major exam date changed in 25 years. Be predictable.

Avoid judging students. Try not to complain that students are not like they used to be. I have heard this for decades. Dewey wrote about this a century ago. This is a dark road to nowhere. Has the pandemic hurt them? Sure. Help them find their power and get back on track. Be gentle and caring but mind the boundaries. Insist on high standards or you further damage their chances of success. They know if you just curve the grades and move on that it hurts them eventually. (unless your exams are just nuts, another issue altogether)

Prerequisites matter. They need help brushing up on those. Thus, I willingly reteach earlier material *briefly* in class. I want *them* to fix their prior learning so they can do the upper-level tasks. I provided such opportunities in Sargent, C. S. 2013. Find it, Fix it, and Thrive: The Impact of Insisting on Proficiency in Prerequisite Knowledge in Intermediate Accounting. *Issues in Accounting Education* 28(3). 581–597. DOI: 10.2308/iace-50456.

CHAPTER 18

JOHN P. THIELMAN, ESQ.
Associate Department Chair
Maurice R. Greenberg School of Risk Science
Robinson College of Business
Georgia State University

What inspired you to teach?

As I moved up the corporate ladder I found that I spent more time training and mentoring lawyers than I spent practicing law. I enjoyed passing on my years of experience with the next generation. I realized I enjoyed teaching. I started as an adjunct professor at Georgia State University in 2010. In Fall 2011, I received an offer to join the faculty full-time and I jumped at the opportunity. It was the students that ultimately inspired me to teach. It is a very rewarding job!

What teaching methods are most helpful in guiding students toward their goals?

My teaching philosophy is to teach the students to become "legally astute" business leaders. Through lectures, class participation, and group projects I apply my real world experience in law, ethics, litigation, Alternative Dispute Resolution, Idea & Asset protection, risk management, torts, and the United States employment environment (hiring, managing, termination, and workplace discrimination) to bring the chapters of the textbook to life for the students. I find tying real life examples to the textbook content helps the student learn and remember the material.

I operate based on three primary areas of focus. First is passion. I model my class presentation after my favorite artist: Bruce Springsteen. I have been a fan for over 40 years. I have seen him in concert every decade since 1980. On stage, he gives 100% every time. He never just goes through the motions. Even though he is singing a song that he wrote 40 years ago, and he sings it over and over while on the road, the fans in the audience paid hard earned money to buy the tickets. They deserve his best. I take that philosophy into the classroom. It may be the one hundredth time I taught this material; it is the students' first and only time. I channel my inner Bruce Springsteen, and always bring the passion.

Second, I make sure not to recycle my exams and that they are always up to date on the current textbook and current law. The trick I use to discipline myself to do this every semester is to use the current students' names in the test questions. This keeps the tests current, and the students get a thrill out of seeing their names on an exam question.

Third, I stay current on the law and bring current legal matters into the classroom. I keep a folder on my computer for every semester. When I come across a current legal matter in the legal press or general press, I will add it to my class folder and add the current legal matter to my lectures. Non-law students find it very helpful when I tie legal concepts to an event that is happening in the news. It makes it real.

What would you like to improve about your teaching?

The technology advances over the past decade have been remarkable. I want to continue to improve how I use new technology to enhance the learning experience.

What skills should be emphasized in high school to succeed in your college class?

I would emphasize to high school students that the skills necessary to succeed in college are universal. No matter what you choose as your major, the key to success is preparation and participation. It is an honor and a privilege to have a seat in a college classroom. Go to class! Participate in class. Do the work. Ask questions.

What is the one thing you wished you would have known when you started your teaching career?/Do you have any last bits of wisdom?

You are the CEO of you. Once you earn your college degree it can never be taken away. The degree will open a lot of doors. You never know what twists and turns your career will take. The knowledge you acquire in college will help you get a job. Your first job will help you get your second job. Your second job will help you get your third job, etc. The key is to always give your best effort at the job you have, and success will follow.

CHAPTER 19

PAUL ULRICH, M.S., PH.D.
Principal Lecturer, Biology
Director, Program for Undergraduate Research
in the Life Sciences
College of Arts & Sciences
Georgia State University

What inspired you to teach?

Central to my interest in teaching were two of my undergraduate professors. When I was 14 years old, I attended my brother's graduation from a small college in upstate New York. My father took me along with him to visit Dr. Ken Boon, the department chair of biology and one of my father's college roommates. I was fascinated by an inside look at a faculty member's office: exam papers strewn about on desks, a stuffed hawk peering down from a shelf, water trickling in an aquarium by the door, and a mysterious back room with who knows what preserved animals. What caught my attention was the energy Dr. Boon exuded as he spoke about biology and his experiences as a zoologist. I've always been infected by a curiosity to learn, and the academic environment seemed just the place! Several years later, I attended the same college and immediately began taking classes from Dr. Boon. He was personally interested in me, helped me figure out a way to anesthetize my pet rat in order to surreptitiously take her with me on a flight home for summer vacation, and was my honors thesis advisor. His investment in me and support of my creativity landed me the research experience that made it possible for me to enter graduate school.

The second influential professor was Dr. Charles Bressler, an English professor. I studied in both his introductory literature course and an advanced writing course. His humor (particularly his feigned disdain of "you scientists"), approachability, and warmth drew me further toward a teaching career. Recently, he moved to Georgia, continues to teach introductory college in an adjunct role, and is a special friend. He was briefly even a colleague at Georgia State University with me. Fancy that!

What teaching methods are most helpful in guiding students toward their goals?

I teach courses ranging from introductory biology for non-science students up to research-intensive laboratory courses. Regardless of the context, I strive to awaken curiosity and wonder in students. To do this, I envision myself as 50% guru, 30% stand-up comedian, and 20% cheerleader. I try to enter the world of a student by surprising them by bridging gaps among course content, the real world, other classes, and their careers. Friendly sarcasm, double-entendre, and lots of smiles are tools I use daily.

My strategies vary for the level of my audience. Students in my biology course for non-science students are a tough crowd, skeptical that biology has anything to do with their degree. The opening of the semester is a key moment to catch their attention. During the first class, I ask them their majors and proceed to draw connections from course content to geopolitics, business, film, psychology, and marketing. A touch of horror helps too. ("Did you know that 16% of those in our class have pinworms living in your intestines?") I fancy students leaving class wondering if the itch they are feeling is a symptom of infection with parasites! Secondly, I reinforce core concepts throughout the semester to explicitly reinforce themes. Examples of this may be explaining diffusion of molecules across a cell membrane when discussing how plants take up water, how oxygen enters our blood, and how our neurons communicate with one another.

Encouragement of students is essential to my approach. I tell my students that I have greater confidence in their potential than they have in themselves, and I call them to rise to the challenge.

For non-science students, I actively break down the lie that they are "just not good at science." My upper division majors working in the lab can grow discouraged by their woeful preparation to work in the real world, and I tailor my mentoring strategy to address their deficits while reminding them of their strengths and gains along the way. At the end of a difficult semester performing late night experiments and weekends in the lab, I facilitate a group debrief session where students tell one another what they appreciate about each other. Recently, my family has begun hosting the entire class at our house for an end of semester potluck. All of these interactions add up, and I hope that they walk away more confident, bold, and mature because of the investment in their personal well-being.

What would you like to improve about your teaching?

I would like to be more concise in content delivery and use time in ways that encourage all students to participate with me in the learning process. A proportion of my success in classrooms relies on humorous anecdotes and personal stories to drive home concepts. However, I tend toward digression and can lose focus of concepts I am trying to reinforce. I would like to refine my approach to recognize the right "dose" of humor and story to reach more students.

Secondly, I would like to learn new strategies for encouraging the silent majority in my introductory courses to take ownership of learning. During the SARS-COV2 pandemic, I flipped my course structure by shifting lecture content to a video format and freeing up class time for discussion, group learning, and problem-solving. Assessment outcomes did not improve with my increased focus on active learning. If anything, average performance sagged. An old problem resurfaced—many students come to class to be taught, not to engage. I would like to find new ways to encourage students to value their own agency for learning and to identify new ways I can interact *directly* with individual students even in large classes.

What skills should be emphasized in high school to succeed in your college class?

The key elements I would like to see emphasized in high school are a combination of personal development and skills. Students should be introduced early to learning as an exploratory process where "failure" is normalized. Fear of getting the answer wrong impedes learning, and students should frequently hear that scientists embrace failure as a way to solve open-ended problems. I would like to see interdependence and initiative as key goals for our high school students. The primary skill that would benefit students in my courses is the ability to create and defend an argument in written form. Students are vaguely aware that they should be able to summarize experimental findings but are generally unaware that scientific process involves a cycle of reading published literature, identifying gaps in scientific literature, and posing experiments that persuasively address these gaps.

What is the one thing you wished you would have known when you started your teaching career?/Do you have any last bits of wisdom?

As a novice teacher, I wish I had known not to personally wrestle through poor student evaluations and DFW rates. Many nights I would go to bed wondering, "What could I have done differently? What did I do wrong?" I have made improvements in my teaching over the years, but I now understand that learning requires the full engagement of both student and instructor. I am responsible for my part of the equation: show compassion to students, listen to, and encourage them. However, I cannot compel them to learn or to mature faster than they are willing regardless of expectations colleagues and my institution may impose.

Keep exploring what you are passionate about! Teaching provides innumerable opportunities for continued learning, and I find that teaching is most rewarding when I am innovating a little bit each semester.

Strategically serve your institution and build your brand around areas of strength. Remind yourself that saying "yes" comes with a cost; it means saying "no" to other areas. There is life outside the ivory tower. Overcommitment by successful teachers will lead to burnout and ultimately compromise more important areas of your life. (*e.g.*, family and health)

CHAPTER 20

MARTA SZABO WHITE, PH.D.
Professor, Clinical, Strategic Management
Robinson College of Business
Georgia State University

What inspired you to teach?

Absolutely NOTHING! I had no idea what I wanted to do. I just stayed in school because I wanted to keep learning ... and then learn even more. Then when I was in the Ph.D. program at Florida State, one of the requirements was to teach the introductory Management class. On my way to the very first class, I walked through the food court and my heel caught on a catsup packet, which in a split-second, splattered all over my light pink suit! Running to the restroom in my matching pink shoes, I was humiliated and horrified. Quickly, I splashed water all over my lovely new suit, and then made a mad dash to the classroom. We connected immediately. There was compassion, but more than anything, an eagerness to learn and share with others. It was love at first meeting. I fell head over heels in love with teaching, becoming more immersed and growing more passionate with each class, with each course, with each study abroad experience, and with each generation of scholars.

What teaching methods are most helpful in guiding students toward their goals?

Here, I am simply going to include my favorite student comment as it is perfectly written:

> It's not often that you get to learn from a professor like Dr. White. It's always a much more enriching and enjoyable experience when you can tell the professor genuinely cares about the students. Dr. White takes a real interest in us as students, and in our success beyond the length of the semester. She is not sim-

ply handing out good grades or helping students for the sake of earning a good evaluation, she is sincerely invested in us and seems to actually enjoy her job. That's not to say she does not take it seriously, as she knows her actions are helping prepare us for our futures, and she does not take that lightly. She knows this class is a crucial building block for business majors, a chance for students to tie together all the concepts they've learned thus far and apply them in a business-like environment. I felt that I not only learned a lot in this course, but was also able to apply what I had learned to think critically through business problems and make more informed, thought-out decisions. Dr. White was stern when she needed to be, but was generally full of personality and had a great sense of humor. She made each lecture as interesting as possible, and gave plenty of relevant examples to help us understand the concepts in a real context. She wanted us to enjoy learning in her class as much as she enjoyed teaching it. She was always available should we need her. That being said, Dr. White was an incredible professor, and the only thing I wish was that there were more professors like her in the program.

What would you like to improve about your teaching?

First, I want to stay as young as my students. This means seeing life through their eyes ... being as exciting, amazing, fascinating, and interesting as whatever they are streaming on their phones. The challenge is to not only be current and knowledgeable, but also compete with social media and whatever they are captivated by on their laptops, phones, etc.

The second challenge is AI. Not that AI could ever replace a dynamic, innovative, interactive professor who is FUN and flexible, cleverly countering student comments. Still, AI is controversial when students masquerade behind it in their work submissions. As educators, we can research how to best manage this dilemma and incorporate it into learning as a productive and useful tool. Several strategies have emerged. My favorite is requiring two papers instead of one. The first is AI-generated, e.g. ChatGPT, and the second is a student-written critique of the first version. Of course, it should be clearly stated that the second paper cannot be a ChatGPT-generated critique of the first one.

What skills should be emphasized in high school to succeed in your college class?

My university's *College to Career Competencies* list is a useful guideline:
- Critical Thinking/Problem Solving
- Oral/Written Communication Skills
- Teamwork/Collaboration
- Digital Technology
- Leadership
- Professionalism/Work Ethics
- Career Management
- Global/Intercultural Fluency

With respect to teaching, be able to teach something to someone else that you are an expert in.

What is the one thing you wished you would have known when you started your teaching career?/Do you have any last bits of wisdom?

Be OPEN!

O—Organized
P—Passionate
E—Energetic
N—Nice

I honestly knew these characteristics to be important even when I first started. Now I know how truly pivotal they are.

CHAPTER 21

Key Takeaway from Each Master Teacher

A few years ago, I asked college juniors and seniors to anonymously list three adjectives that describe an effective teacher. The results were predictable, at least to me: Adaptive; Articulate; Dedicated; Empathetic (top response); Energetic; Engaging (top response); Enthusiastic; Helpful; Immersive; Knowledgeable; Organized; Passionate (top response); Patient; Positive; Practical; Reliable; and Versatile.

I hope you agree that the Master Teachers in this book embody many of these qualities, including the top responses: Empathetic, Engaging, and Passionate. To capture their key takeaways in this book, I selected quotes that were most impactful to me:

Diana S. Barber

"I use numerous techniques to stay engaged with students, including intelligent agents that will automatically send email messages to students if they miss a quiz or assignment, as a reminder that I am available to assist and that their success is important to me."

Jordan (Jody) Blanke

"I like to teach by example. I think it is much easier to understand an idea if you can see it in action, rather than merely in the abstract. Quite often you can discuss the nuances of the topic by simply varying the facts of the example."

Yelena Abalmazova Chan

"Encourage students to explore all careers, classes, and topics that interest them. I really believe it's a duty we have as instructors.

I see some students tied to a major just because that's what they chose based on pretty much no research or experience, and they clearly have no passion for it. There is nothing wrong with majoring in accounting but consider interning at a bakery if that's something that piques their interest. Sometimes hearing that from an authority figure like a college professor is encouraging and gives students the permission to explore outside the box."

Evaristo Fernando Doria

"I am enthusiastic about expanding my efforts to create more cross-border interdisciplinary learning experiences. Such experiences not only prompt participants to critically analyze novel ideas and challenges but also encourage them to delve into the intricate intersections of various fields of study while developing their global mindset."

L. Gregory (Greg) Henley

"It's very important that I reach the students on their level. If I can get their attention, then I can teach them. Improving my teaching requires that I get constructive feedback to ensure that what I'm doing is working."

Leila Lawlor

"If you have chosen to teach, you have chosen to place students at the center of your professional universe. Tell them. They will appreciate knowing how much you want them to thrive, to enjoy your teaching, and to meet their academic and professional goals. As you get to know your students, they will surely appreciate your interest in their lives and goals."

Laura E. Meyers

"Unlearn. We need to deconstruct what we know and consider how we learned this and who it favors. Unlearning is one way to reduce bias and, in turn, harm. Unlearning can lead to allyship (and more) which is beneficial to our students (and us) in 'becoming' educators. Aren't we always growing and becoming?"

Isabelle N. Monlouis

"Students need to learn how to fail forward. Learning to fail and learning from failure, with no loss of enthusiasm. Trying again, knowing this time, you are trying with the benefit of experience so you will be more successful. ... And we need to learn how to teach without penalizing 'failure' but instead recontextualizing it as gathering valuable information to make their next attempt more successful."

Benita Harris Moore

"If you are offered a new responsibility that is not 'pure teaching,' be open to it. The new opportunity may or may not take you from the classroom but may open doors that are different than you could have imagined. Don't be afraid to accept these opportunities. My 40+ years in education was enhanced because I said 'yes' to opportunities that were presented to me, even if the new challenge was outside of my comfort zone."

Carol Springer Sargent

"My most popular technique to this day was the result of a learning experiment with a struggling student. ... I asked him if he would just give me the commercial breaks during Law and Order. (his favorite show) He agreed. I created three-minute coaching videos that taught a core idea in each video. I focused on one foundational idea that, if missed, would make the rest of the chapter impossible. The 'just three minutes' was a wild success."

John P. Thielman

"I make sure not to recycle my exams and that they are always up to date on the current textbook and current law. The trick I use to discipline myself to do this every semester is to use the current students' names in the test questions. This keeps the tests current, and the students get a thrill out of seeing their names on an exam question."

Paul Ulrich

"Encouragement of students is essential to my approach. I tell my students that I have greater confidence in their potential than they have in themselves, and I call them to rise to the challenge. For non-science students, I actively break down the lie that they are 'just not good at science.'"

Marta Szabo White

"Be OPEN! Organized, Passionate, Energetic, Nice. I honestly knew these characteristics to be important even when I first started. Now I know how truly pivotal they are."

And finally, from the author

Make your classes interactive with activities solving real world problems. Encourage students to be confident in their fact-based opinions and continually challenge or "teach the teacher." For example, in my Internet Law class, students know more than me about emerging technologies such as AI, blockchain, crypto, and NFTs. While I can teach the legal limits of technology, it is the energy of students which carries this class, as they educate me. This shift in roles grew my skills as a college professor. Ultimately, I want my classes to not only be student-centered but life-centered as well.

EPILOGUE

"I live by two words: tenacity and gratitude."
—Henry Winkler

From time to time, I reflect on my teaching career, looking to capture my sentiment in the moment in one word. Recently, I watched an interview with Henry Winkler as he discussed the ups and many downs of his acting career after the hit television show, *Happy Days,* ended in 1984. The word that stuck with me was that he was grateful for everything. Grateful. Work hard and be grateful. During the ups and the downs. Appreciate current and former students and colleagues, and all of the people you've met along the way.

I am grateful to the professors interviewed for this book. Unknown to them, they elevated my game as I edited their chapters. When students ask me about time management techniques, I tell them to be strategic and efficient with their time. To learn how and when to say no. But if I listened to my own advice, I likely would've passed on a great opportunity. As I was re-reading about the amazing work these Master Teachers are doing with their students, I was inspired to say yes.

This led me to take on the task of recruiting and coaching a team of three students to compete in a three-day international mediation competition hosted by a neighboring university. These students weren't in my Consumer Law class, had zero exposure to mediation training, and went up against many students who were Conflict Resolution majors. They had five weeks to learn how to mediate a dispute and switch roles from mediator to advocate to client in mock mediation sessions. The same amount of training time that Rocky had to fight world champion, Apollo Creed. The students worked hard and performed admirably. They demonstrated skill, patience, empathy, and poise under pressure, and articulated reflective insights.

Author Dan Millman once said: "The journey is what brings us happiness, not the destination." I am grateful to the students who sacrificed their time during this adventure to learn and experience something new. In turn, these types of interactions facilitate my growth as a professor and person. All of which motivates me to seek out my next quest.

APPENDIX

APPENDIX A
First Day of Class Story: Youthful "Offenders" (A Transcription)

My classroom syllabus says: No legal advice questions! But I still get calls from students, sometimes when it's too late—after they have a court date.

You know how you get one phone call before you get hauled off to prison? Well, I was in the office and got this call from "Steve:"

"Help me Perry they're taking me awaaaaaaaaaaaay!"

I'm like:

"Where the heck are youuuuuuuuuuuuuuuuu?"

"The DeKalb Detention Center."

Yeah. So I had a night class. After my night class at 10 o'clock at night, I'm on the highway getting off at Memorial Drive and there's a McDonald's, a Dunkin', and a huge building with people banging on the window screaming:

"Get me outta here!"

And I walk in there with my squeaky voice:

"Uh, I'm here to see my student."

And they're like:

"You're just a lowly prof; get outta here."

So I fumble around in my wallet looking for an attorney Bar card, and I find a CVS card, a Costco card, a ticket to the Vatican, and finally I find the right one. (*all displayed on the doc cam*)

They put me in this bright white room with a huge window overlooking the jail. And by the way, it's a very clean facility if you're looking to visit or even stay for a bit. So anyway they bring out my student, on the other side of the glass, in his orange jumpsuit and handcuffed and he is sitting there and he is really, really looking distraught.

Now remember I told you my experience is as a commercial litigator. I never did criminal law so my knowledge of that is from TV. So I drew off that experience, and I put my hand up on the glass with my fingers spread apart.

And Steve's looking at it. And looking at it. And I don't move an inch. And then he put his hand on mine and smiled!

The TV hand thing works!

(*still speaking to my class*)

Why do I tell you this story?

Here's what my student did. He was driving excessively, over 100 miles an hour. Raise your hand if you've done that. That's not good. Okay.

He got a ticket for reckless driving, which is a misdemeanor. Here was his real crime: Being young, goofy, and showing up to court without an attorney. The judge threw him in jail for ten days. If he had an attorney, what likely would've happened was some kind of plea deal with no prison time.

So now here he is sitting in jail and I had to get him a criminal attorney that he'd have to pay a whole lot more than if he had one in the first place. That attorney somehow got him out in three days.

In this class, we will discuss when you need an attorney and when you do not need an attorney. Before a problem gets really big, that's when you need an attorney. And we will talk about a lot of those scenarios. We'll talk about you as a businessperson, but we'll also talk about your rights as an individual, and how to apply the law to each situation.

And be careful, since the judge has a lot of power. Always remember: It's good to be the judge.

Another time, my student, "Betty," was arrested after attending a Tone Lōc concert. She unknowingly wound up as a passenger in an allegedly stolen vehicle. The next morning, I received a phone call from Betty's grandmother asking me to bail out her granddaughter.

After getting the cash from grandma, I went to the county jail where the guard took me to a dim and dank holding cell. I was looking all lawyerly with my blue pinstripe suit and sharp leather shoes and briefcase. Another guard escorted Betty into the cell. Her hair was disheveled, a stiletto was missing from one shoe, and she looked frazzled. I said:

"Betty, we have two options, I could get you out of here now, or"—as I reached into my briefcase—"right now, you can take the Midterm Exam that you missed last week."

Betty's reaction?

"Get me the frick out of here!"

Ninety minutes after the exam commenced, Betty was set free. I'll let you judge for yourself how true the prior sentence is.

Always remember: It's good to be the prof.

In the above anecdotes, I am not suggesting that college professors show up to jail at 10:00 p.m. or at a grandma's home in the wee hours of the morning. Rather, my point is to let students know that they can contact you in an emergency to guide them to appropriate help and resources.

The Steve story can be viewed on my YouTube channel @Perry_Binder.
www.youtube.com/watch?v=UM4qK52P__Q
"Professor Perry Binder's Student Prisoner Story"
(*3-minute clip*)

APPENDIX B
Spelling/Grammatical Errors in Student Papers

(Syllabus excerpt—The value of proofreading)
    A faulty (faculty) member—maybe the student got this one right!
    File a mew (new) motion
    Going to trail (trial)
    Lead (led) to believe
    Singing (Signing) an Agreement
    The Compliant (Complaint)
    Tired (Tried) to flee the scene
    Breech (Breach) of contract
    Break (Breach) of contract
    Stature (Statute) of limitations
    Statue (Statute) of limitations
    Legal principals (principles)
    The principle point (principal)
    Recover principle (principal), court costs, and interest

Awkward Sentences

<u>Student version</u>: According to my viewpoint, the case was pretty straightforward with the easiness of issue involved between the parties.

<u>My version</u>: In my view, the case was straightforward with easy issues facing the parties.

<u>Student version</u>: The attorney briefly insinuated the relationship of two of the board members and made it seem like they had previously made a pact with each other.

<u>My version</u>: The attorney insinuated that two board members previously made a pact.

APPENDIX C
Sample Term Sheet

Intellectual Property: intangible property rights. Huh? Mostly governed by federal statutes

I. Copyrights

Elements of Infringement
- Ownership
- Defendant's access to your work
- Copying/substantial similarity
- Damages

What's copyrightable? Not short ideas. The original, tangible expression of _____.

    Examples:

    When is it copyrighted?
    Do I need the © symbol on my work?
    Poor man's copyright.

Advantages of registration with the U.S. Copyright Office*
- within 3 months of producing work
- attorney fees
- election of actual or statutory damages

<u>Defenses</u>
- Permission
- Public domain
- Fair use
- Parody

    Lasts life of author plus __ years
    Work for hire or anonymous work: shorter period of __ years from date of publication or __ years from date of creation

---

* copyright.gov

What is Work for Hire? (Remember this from the Contracts material?)
- Who owns the IP?
- Protecting software?

II. Patents

Utility: non-obvious, novel, useful
Plant
Design: ornamental
Application process
- Claims section

Patents last __ years (Design lasts __)

III. Trade Secrets

Defined:

IV. Trademarks:
They last forever IF you use it continuously in commerce AND renew it

Trademarks and Service marks protect:
- Trade names
- Logos (can copyright your logo too)
- Slogans
- Trade dress

Levels of protection
1: Common law—use TM and SM
2: State—use TM and SM
- secretary of state's office: renewable every __ years
3: federal
- renewable every __ years
- Intent to use (not at state level): use it within 6 months
- ® symbol
4: international

Infringement—proving confusion in the minds of the public
Treble damages if intentional infringement

Strength of mark
Distinctive
Secondary meaning—Windows
Generic

Invention Depicted in Chapter 6

The most common student guesses include amoeba, artist palette, boomerang, flying saucer, game console, and neck pillow. But of course, the invention is a household necessity, the can opener.

APPENDIX D
Sample Module for Interactive Classroom Discussions

Outside of class, read the instructions for each module and be prepared to discuss them in class. Module information and discussions are testable.

Note: Most of these modules are intentionally written vaguely to generate a wide range of reactions and solutions. They are designed to promote critical thinking and explore your soft communication skills. Your participation in these activities is expected.

Products Liability and Ethics Module

(*Break up into student teams of three for 15 minutes*)

Everyone watch (before the in-class session) the case video: GM/Moseley Trial (48 minutes)

www.youtube.com/watch?v=QU_uTuWmtHA

(Moseley vs. General Motors: A Son's Death: Is GM at Fault?)

In class, react to these questions:
1: Give your general impressions of the attorneys.
   a. Is there value in seeking local counsel?
2: Which theory do you believe—the plaintiff's or the defendant's? Why?
3: The engineer testifying for the plaintiff used to testify on behalf of the defendant in similar cases. Assess his credibility as the plaintiff's witness in the current case.
4: In the video deposition, a former company employee discussed destroyed documents. What role did corporate ethics play in the size of the jury verdict?
5: If your deposition (*depo*) were being taken by the plaintiff's attorney in this case (assume that you are a current company employee), what general tips would the attorney *defending* the depo give you? Would the preparation be the same for a video depo, as opposed to a transcribed depo?
   a. Give an example in this case where prior sworn testimony was used at trial to *impeach* a witness.
6: Was the jury's verdict sound? Explain.
7: What questions were left unanswered for you in this case?

APPENDIX E
Using AI to Develop Classroom Modules

The first ChatGPT 3.5 prompt: **"Mediation Simulation Scenario."**
Results:

Facts: John is a landlord who owns a rental property in a residential area. He leased the property to Jane, a tenant, for a one-year lease. The lease agreement stated that the tenant is responsible for maintaining the yard and keeping it in good condition.

During the tenancy, John observed that the yard was not being properly maintained by Jane. He sent her a written notice, asking her to fix the issues, but Jane did not comply with the request.

John then hired a professional landscaping company to fix the yard and charged Jane for the cost of the service.

Jane argues that the yard was not in a bad condition when she moved in, and she has been doing her best to maintain it. She also claims that John did not give her enough notice before hiring the landscaping company and charging her for the service. She believes that John is trying to unfairly take advantage of her.

On the other hand, John argues that he had given Jane sufficient notice to fix the issues with the yard, and he had no other option but to hire a professional landscaping company to maintain it.

He believes that it is reasonable to charge Jane for the cost of the service since it was her responsibility to maintain the yard in good condition.

The parties have tried to resolve the issue amongst themselves, but they have not been successful. They have agreed to participate in mediation to try and find a mutually satisfactory solution.

Next, I typed in ChatGPT **"fair compromise for mediation simulation"**

Here's a possible fair compromise for the mediation simulation scenario:

After hearing both sides of the dispute, as a mediator, I suggest the following compromise:

John agrees to waive the cost of the landscaping service that he charged Jane, but Jane agrees to take responsibility for maintaining the yard going forward. John will provide Jane with a written notice if he observes any issues with the yard, and Jane agrees to fix the issues within a reasonable time frame.

In addition, John agrees to give Jane a reasonable amount of time to fix any issues with the yard before taking any further action, and Jane agrees to promptly address any issues brought to her attention.

Both parties agree to sign a written agreement outlining these terms and to abide by them. This agreement will be binding and enforceable.

This compromise allows John to have a tenant who will take responsibility for maintaining the yard, and it allows Jane to avoid paying for the landscaping service. It also provides a clear understanding of expectations for both parties and promotes future cooperation between them.

Then I hit **"Regenerate Response"**

John (the landlord) and Jane (the tenant) agree to split the cost of the professional landscaping service equally, with each party paying 50% of the total cost. Moving forward, Jane agrees to maintain the yard in good condition as per the lease agreement. If there are any issues with the yard in the future, John agrees to provide Jane with a written notice specifying the problem and allowing her a reasonable time to fix it before hiring a professional landscaping company. Both parties agree to communicate with each other in a respectful and timely manner and to avoid any further disputes related to the yard maintenance.

Again, I hit **"Regenerate Response"**

A possible fair compromise for this mediation simulation could be:
1. John agrees to waive the cost of the professional landscaping company that he hired to fix the yard.
2. ane agrees to take responsibility for maintaining the yard in good condition going forward and will do her best to improve its current state.
3. Jane will also pay a reduced amount to John as compensation for the inconvenience caused by the poor condition of the yard during her tenancy.

4. Both parties will agree to communicate with each other promptly in case of any issues or concerns regarding the rental property.

This compromise allows Jane to take responsibility for the yard's maintenance going forward while also recognizing the inconvenience caused to John by the poor condition of the yard. It also avoids the need for John to take legal action to recover the cost of the landscaping company and encourages better communication between the parties.

I added a few common facts:
- The landscaping cost the landlord $800.
- Landlord got three estimates: 600/700/800.
- Went with 800 because he worked once with this company.

Then because it's important to have separate facts for each party, I also added:

Additional Landlord Facts:
- Landlord is willing to lower his ask to $600.
- See how it goes—firmly doesn't want to go below $400.
- CONFIDENTIAL: Jane is a very good tenant—scared to lose her/hassle to re-lease the place.

Additional Tenant Facts:
- Tenant is willing to offer $150 for landscaping
- See how it goes—firmly doesn't want to go above $300
- CONFIDENTIAL: Jane is very scared that her lease will not be renewed and is afraid of going to court.

APPENDIX F
AI-Generated Demand Letter Assignment—
Do You Have a Potential Legal Dispute?

Think about any past or present contract dispute, landlord dispute, company dispute, auto dispute, medical dispute, dispute with a friend over a loan, or any other dispute where the recovery of money is involved. To respect everyone's privacy, do not divulge any personal information and change the name/s of defendant/s.

This is an exercise to show you that you do not need an attorney to write a powerful demand letter. You have Artificial Intelligence to guide you. Below, I demonstrate how I wrote a demand letter using FREE ChatGPT 3.5.

At the top of your letter, put your name and "Real Case" or "Made Up Case" or "Part Real/Part Made Up" (I'll explain further in class). If it is a real case, this assignment might motivate you to take action.

This is a required but easy assignment. It is <u>ungraded</u> for two reasons:
1. You are using AI to write it; and
2. It serves as a first draft if you choose to complete Individual Project A. I will provide feedback on this letter that may be useful for that graded project.

Up to 10 points will be deducted from your project grade if you do not post the letter in a timely fashion. Upload it to Assessment/Assignment in iCollege.

"Write" a properly formatted demand letter (single-spaced/double-spaced between paragraphs) using the Chronology approach (see Sample Demand Letter in iCollege). Remember to be as detailed as possible on names, dates, and facts. If it is a real case, have you kept all relevant documentation? If so, refer to everything in your letter (but do not upload attachments).

I want your letter to be as good as the sample letters I provide in class. (No page length requirement)

These are the actual chronological prompts I used to create a "Made Up" Demand Letter in ChatGPT 3.5:

- Write demand letter landlord in Atlanta won't fix air conditioning
- Add six dates over a ten day period that tenant called or emailed landlord
- Now put those dates in the body of the demand letter
- Add in May 4: I got three estimates from a repair company attached to this letter
  - Did not do it
  - I then hit the Regenerate button which got it done
- Use real names John Smith is the tenant Jill Jones is the landlord
  - It did it!
- Now add a statement at the end if I do not hear back by May 12 hire third party under repair and deduct law

FINAL PRODUCT: I formatted and added: Name/Address/Date of the letter and (via email and hand-delivered to leasing office)

Made Up Case: Perry Binder

John Smith
Address
May 11, 2023
(via email and hand-delivered to leasing office)

Jill Jones
Address

Dear Ms. Jones:

I am writing to express my dissatisfaction with the current condition of the air conditioning system in my apartment located at 123 Main St. As you are aware, the air conditioning system has been malfunctioning for several weeks now and despite numerous requests for repair, no action has been taken.

As evidence of my attempts to communicate with you regarding this matter, I would like to reference the following dates when I, John Smith, contacted you to report the air conditioning malfunction:

1. May 1, 2023: I called you to report air conditioning malfunction.
2. May 3, 2023: I sent an email to you requesting repair of air conditioning system.
3. May 4, 2023: I obtained three repair estimates from a professional company, which are attached to this letter.
4. May 5, 2023: I called you to follow up on repair request.
5. May 7, 2023: I sent a second email to you requesting immediate action to fix the air conditioning system.
6. May 8, 2023: I called you again to inquire about repair timeline.
7. May 10, 2023: I sent a third email to you demanding immediate repair of the air conditioning system.

I would like to remind you that as my landlord, it is your responsibility to ensure that the apartment is in a habitable condition and that all necessary repairs are promptly addressed. The lack of action on your part has made it extremely uncomfortable for me to live in the apartment, especially during the hot summer months.

I have taken the initiative to obtain three estimates from a professional repair company for the repair of the air conditioning system, which are attached to this letter. I demand that you, Ms. Jones, immediately take action to fix the air conditioning system in my apartment and provide me with a timeline for when the repairs will be completed. If the repairs are not completed within a reasonable time frame, I will have no other choice but to take legal action to enforce my rights as a tenant.

If I do not hear back from you by May 12, 2023, I will be forced to hire a third-party repair company and deduct the cost of the repair from my rent under the "repair and deduct" law in Georgia.

I would appreciate your prompt attention to this matter. Please feel free to contact me if you have any questions or concerns.

Sincerely,
John Smith

APPENDIX G
Project Based on Demand Letter

Part I:

Revise your Demand Letter per my feedback and upload it with Parts II & III on one Word document. (the revised letter will be graded)

Part II:

Refer to the Statement of Claim below [not included here]—Copy and paste it into your Word document. Fill it out and label it Part II.
- Make sure the case style is accurate.
- What are your damages? Be specific.
- Make sure you know if the defendant is a corporation with a fictitious name: XYZ, Inc. d/b/a Smelly Shoes.
- Is it a Georgia or out-of-state corporation? ecorp.sos.ga.gov/BusinessSearch

Part III:

A. Assume that your texts, phone calls, and demand letters have been ignored and you've exhausted all non-litigation remedies. Would you consider filing a small claims action in this matter? What are the pros and cons? Be specific.

As you think about Part III.A., apply Perry's Three Steps:
1. *Do You Have a Good Case? Explain. Does the other side have a reasonable defense?*
2. *Can You Collect Your Money If You Win?* (*Is the defendant solvent?*)
3. *Is the dispute based on a contract or statute which contains an attorneys' fee clause?*

B. How confident do you feel about utilizing the small claims court process in this case? Explain. What are your biggest fears (if any) about pursuing the matter in court?

Parts III.A. and III.B. combined must be 3 full pages double-spaced.

APPENDIX H
Incorporating AI with Minor Tweak to Assignment

How the Internet Changed Professions

<u>Understatement</u>: The internet has changed how we do business, whether in the United States or worldwide.

Section A. Use a free AI tool (I use the free version of ChatGPT 3.5)—figure out what prompt to use.

Choose ANY profession. Discuss how the internet has improved, complicated, revolutionized, and/or adversely impacted the profession and the people working in that profession.

(500–700-ish words)

Section B. Do not use AI

In your own words, reflect on the information in Section A by agreeing or disagreeing with any of the points. Then, conduct research on the web: Give specific examples of how the profession operated successfully in a pre-internet era versus a post-internet era. In addition, identify how the legal knowledge learned in this course will benefit you if working in that profession.

(3 full pages)

Section C. Do not use AI

Find two cases in the news where some aspect of the profession relating to the internet is currently being litigated (or from the past that was litigated) in court. (whether at the pre-trial, trial, or appellate stage) Give the facts of the case, the main issue/s involved, which party or parties you believe will prevail (and why) and how you believe this case will impact the future of the profession and/or the people working in the profession.

(3 full pages)

Instructions

1. Double-spaced, one-inch margins, 12-point font—Times New Roman or Arial. See page length below (no longer, no shorter)
2. Type your name at the top of the paper.
3. Numbered Footnotes, if any, should be included on an additional page—I prefer this to a Resource List.
4. Label each section: Section A, B, C

ChapGPT 3.5-Generated Responses

Prompt: Explain how the internet has changed the music profession beginning in 1995

The advent of the internet has revolutionized the music profession in countless ways since its widespread adoption in the mid-1990s. In this essay, I will explore some of the most significant ways in which the internet has changed the music industry over the past 25 years.

One of the most significant changes brought about by the internet is the democratization of music production and distribution. Prior to the internet, the ability to produce and distribute music was largely controlled by a small group of record labels and radio stations.

However, with the rise of digital audio workstations (DAWs) and online distribution platforms like iTunes and Spotify, anyone with a computer and an internet connection can produce and distribute their own music. This has led to a proliferation of new artists and genres that might not have had a chance to succeed under the old model.

Another major change brought about by the internet is the rise of social media and its impact on music marketing and promotion. Social media platforms like Twitter, Instagram, and TikTok have given artists and their teams direct access to fans and potential fans, allowing them to build and maintain relationships with their audience in ways that were previously impossible. Social media has also made it easier for artists to collaborate with one another, regardless of their geographic location, leading to a greater diversity of musical styles and collaborations.

The internet has also disrupted the traditional revenue streams for musicians, both positively and negatively. On the one hand, the rise of streaming services like Spotify has made music more accessible to consumers than ever before. However, the shift from physical album sales to streaming has drastically reduced the amount of money that artists make from their music. This has forced many artists to rely more heavily on touring and merchandise sales to make a living. On the other hand, the internet has also made it easier for artists to monetize their music through channels like YouTube and Patreon, which allow them to earn money directly from their fans.

The internet has also had a significant impact on the way that music is consumed. Prior to the internet, consumers had limited options for discovering new music beyond what was played on the radio or available in record stores. However, with the rise of streaming services and online music communities, consumers now have access to an almost infinite variety of music from around the world. This has led to a greater diversity of musical tastes and styles, as well as increased demand for niche genres and subcultures.

Another way that the internet has changed the music industry is through its impact on the live music experience. Social media and online ticketing platforms like Eventbrite and Ticketmaster have made it easier for fans to discover and attend live music events, leading to a greater demand for live music. This has had a positive impact on the touring industry, allowing artists to reach new audiences and generate more revenue from ticket sales. However, it has also led to a greater emphasis on spectacle and production value in live performances, as artists compete for attention in a crowded market.

Finally, the internet has also had a significant impact on the way that musicians and their audiences interact with one another. Online communities and fan forums have given fans a platform to discuss and share their favorite music, as well as interact with the artists themselves. This has created a more intimate and personal relationship between musicians and their fans, as well as a greater sense of community and belonging among music lovers.

In conclusion, the internet has had a profound impact on the music profession since its widespread adoption in the mid-1990s. From the democratization of music production and distribution to the rise of social media and the disruption of traditional revenue streams, the internet has fundamentally changed the way that music is created, distributed, consumed, and experienced. While these changes have brought both opportunities and challenges for musicians and the music industry as a whole, there is no doubt that the internet will continue to **[ChatGPT word limit cut off here]**

Prompt: AI improves, complicates, revolutionizes, and has a positive and negative impact on the legal profession

Absolutely, artificial intelligence (AI) has had a multifaceted impact on the legal profession, both positive and negative. Let's break down how AI has influenced various aspects of the legal field:

1. Efficiency and Automation: AI-powered tools can handle tasks like document review, contract analysis, and due diligence much faster and with higher accuracy than human lawyers. This frees up legal professionals to focus on more complex and strategic aspects of their work.
2. Legal Research: AI can significantly speed up the process of legal research by quickly identifying relevant case law, statutes, and regulations. This helps lawyers build stronger arguments and provide more informed advice to clients.
3. Predictive Analytics: AI algorithms can analyze large volumes of data to predict case outcomes, jury decisions, and legal strategies. This enables lawyers to make more informed decisions and advise clients on potential outcomes.
4. Access to Justice: AI-powered chatbots and online platforms can provide basic legal information to individuals who can't afford traditional legal services, thereby improving access to justice for marginalized populations.
5. Risk Management: AI can identify potential legal risks in contracts and agreements, helping businesses and individuals make more informed decisions and avoid potential legal disputes.

Negative Impacts:
1. Job Disruption: The automation of tasks like document review and legal research could lead to a reduction in demand for junior lawyers who traditionally handle these tasks. This

could potentially lead to job losses or changes in the nature of legal work.
2. Data Privacy and Ethics: The use of AI in legal practice raises concerns about the privacy and security of sensitive legal information. Lawyers must ensure that AI tools adhere to ethical and legal standards when processing such data.
3. Bias and Fairness: AI algorithms can inherit biases present in the data they're trained on, potentially leading to biased outcomes in legal decision-making. This could exacerbate existing disparities in the legal system.
4. Loss of Human Judgment: While AI can analyze data and provide predictions, it may lack the nuanced human judgment required for complex legal cases that involve emotion, ethics, and social considerations.
5. Complexity and Dependence: The adoption of AI technologies requires legal professionals to understand and manage these tools effectively. There's a risk of becoming overly dependent on AI, potentially reducing critical thinking and analytical skills.

Complications and Revolutions:
1. New Legal Challenges: The use of AI raises novel legal questions, such as who is responsible if an AI-powered legal tool makes an error, or how to regulate AI in the legal industry to ensure ethical use.
2. Changing Legal Education: The legal curriculum may need to adapt to include training in understanding and working with AI technologies, ensuring that future lawyers are prepared for the evolving legal landscape.
3. Alternative Legal Services: AI has enabled the rise of alternative legal service providers, such as legal tech startups. This has revolutionized the way legal services are delivered, challenging traditional law firms.

In summary, AI has brought about significant changes to the legal profession, improving efficiency and accessibility while introducing new challenges related to ethics, bias, and human judgment. The legal industry must find a balance between leveraging AI's benefits and addressing its potential drawbacks to ensure a fair, effective, and just legal system.

APPENDIX I
Short Team Project

Discovery Ethics and Attorney-Client Privilege

Procedure
1. Upload the paper to our LMS
2. The group will turn in one paper, Times New Roman or Arial, double-spaced, unless otherwise indicated.

How Projects Will Be Graded

Your project will be graded on the following items:
a. how much thought went into the paper and how well you organize your thoughts, research, and arguments
b. whether your information is factually correct and your legal arguments are sound, logical, and well-reasoned, based on the topics
c. how well you follow the instructions
d. spelling and grammar

Team members will receive the same grade on the Team Project. If a team member does not meet his or her responsibilities on the project, it is initially up to the group to resolve the problem. The Instructor is available to mediate but is the last resort for dispute resolution.

Hypothetical Facts

Last year, Sharon Smith filed a lawsuit in Fulton County State Court against The Company (TC), a Georgia corporation, alleging injuries caused by TC's product. Assume that attorneys for Smith have begun the discovery process and that you are a middle manager at TC. Your supervisor puts you in charge of gathering all documents requested by the plaintiff (which include all interoffice memoranda concerning TC's allegedly defective product in the Smith case) in their Request for Production of Documents. These documents will then be passed on to in-house and outside counsel to screen them for relevance and privileged material.

In the course of gathering these documents, you come across a *smoking gun* memorandum written last September to your previous supervisor (who is no longer with the company) by a TC senior vice president who is still with the company. The memo, which you show to your current supervisor, says, in part: *"Just spoke with outside counsel.* The Smith attorneys are threatening litigation; destroy all documents."*

The next day, your supervisor orally informs you: *"Just met with in-house counsel. Good news—she agrees that the memo doesn't fit the parameters of plaintiff's discovery request. Please get rid of it discreetly."* Though you lack legal training, your gut feeling is that the document may fit the request.

Your Objectives: 1) to do the ethical thing; 2) while protecting your bright future in the company; and 3) while protecting TC from further liability.

Goal: Achieve ALL three (3) objectives. However, you MUST do the ethical thing, whatever that is.

A. <u>Teams will write a short memo</u> (1–2 paragraphs for each question below, unless otherwise specified) on the following questions (single space/double space between paragraphs):

1. Is the smoking gun memo covered by the attorney-client privilege?
2. What is a litigation hold, and when does it become applicable?
3. Which people in the company will you speak with as you figure out a way out of this dilemma? Describe the course of action you've devised to resolve this problem and achieve your three objectives. Be specific. (3–4 paragraphs)
4. Assume you are the middle manager in this case and the plaintiff is planning to take your deposition. What questions will you have for TC's attorneys? Would you seek your own attorney?

---

*Note: This is the same outside attorney handling TC's present defense.

B. <u>Include as a separate document</u>:

Team/s will write a short interoffice memo to your current supervisor on this matter. (the person who told you to get rid of the document) The content of the memo is up to the team, as you figure out your solution above, and can be as brief as you deem necessary.

APPENDIX J
Team Project Peer Evaluation Form

Everyone fill out a form and hands in separately

Your Name _____
- On a 1–10 scale (with 10 being 100% effort), rate the quality and extent of your contribution to the project. ____

Complete this form for each team member below. Responses will be kept confidential.

1. Name of team member being evaluated _____
Rate this team member on the following items. (5 is highest, 3 is average and 1 is lowest)
- Did fair share of the work.
  5 4 3 2 1
- Cooperated with other team members and was willing to compromise.
  5 4 3 2 1
- Completed tasks on schedule.
  5 4 3 2 1
- I would work with this person in the future.
  5 4 3 2 1

On a 1–10 scale (with 10 being 100% effort):
- Rate the quality and extent of this team member's contribution _____

2. Name of team member being evaluated _____
   Etc.

APPENDIX K
Sample Essay Exam Question and Model Answer

Assume that everyone in our class is a cast member (the "Cast") of a new reality television show, Legal Environment 101, set in a huge mansion where the Cast gets to live, sleep, and study. The producers of the show place $1,000,000 in the Cast bank account, to spend at its discretion on house-related needs. At the first house meeting, the Cast agrees that everyone lives like slobs, so it collectively decides to seek out the best home cleaner in the business.

The Cast interviews Bob the Cleaner, who earns $1,000,000/year cleaning several messy mansions nearby. Bob and the Cast sign an exclusive contract where Bob is to clean the Cast's house five days/week for one full year. Thereafter, Bob informs his current clients that he can't clean their homes because of this contract. The Cast puts a provision in the contract stating that Bob must work the full year to receive the money, otherwise, he receives no compensation. Bob agrees to this stipulation, though the Cast does not explain its reason in the contract.

Bob gets to work right away, with a mop, bucket, and gritty determination. For the next six months, Bob does a stellar job. In fact, several house members have raved about Bob on Facebook, and not one house member has registered a complaint about Bob's work. The next day, Bob requests a house meeting with the Cast. With cameras rolling, Bob looks at everyone and in a dramatic moment of television history states: "You are all a bunch of slobs and I quit today. You owe me $500,000 right now."

Discuss all legal issues involved and conclude whether Bob would win if he filed a Complaint against the Cast and producers of Legal Environment 101.

Model Essay Answer

Plaintiff, Bob, may have actions at law and in "equity." He will sue both the Cast and producers of Legal Environment 101, as detailed be-

low. In the Discovery process of the lawsuit, he might find more information as to the liability of the parties.
- An Action at Law is a cause of action which derives from traditional British common law, where parties usually may seek a remedy before a judge or jury.
- Equity Actions were derived from England's Chancery courts, and serve to remedy or supplement the limitations of common law. In most cases, only a judge may hear Equity claims with concepts of fairness.

Plaintiff, Bob's Possible Causes of Action v. The Cast and Producers ("Defendants")
   A. Breach of Contract (Action at Law)
- Bob will file a Breach of Contract claim. However, the face of the contract says that he must work one year to collect $1,000,000, so he likely would lose this claim.
   B. Quantum Meruit (Equity)
- If Bob cannot recover for Breach of Contract, he may ask the judge for the value of his services. (Quantum Meruit) By showing the judge that he worked for six months, he will sue "off the contract" and argue that his services are worth half of $1,000,000, or $500,000. In support of his claim, he can present earnings for previous years. In addition, he can introduce evidence that none of the Cast members were dissatisfied with his services and in fact, many of them gave rave reviews of his work on Facebook.
   C. Promissory Estoppel (Equity)
- Promissory Estoppel is when someone relies on a promise and is harmed. In reliance on the Cast's promise, Bob signed an exclusive contract and had to give up his cleaning appointments with other clients. If Bob is now unable to regain his old business clients, he may be able to argue that his reliance on the exclusive contract led to lost income.

Possible Defense for the Cast/Producers
   The One-Year Stipulation
- The Defendants will assert that the one-year stipulation is unambiguous and is a condition precedent to the contract. (something a party is supposed to do as stated in the contract

before something else can occur) Neither the fact pattern nor the contract provides further information on why the one-year clause was inserted into the contract.

Conclusions
1. Bob will likely lose his Breach of Contract claim, but should prevail on his Quantum Meruit claim. (with the amount of damages determined by the judge)
2. The fact pattern does not provide enough information to assess the merits of the Equity claim for Promissory Estoppel, or the Defendants' One-Year Stipulation defense.

APPENDIX L
Calculating Course Grades for Graduating Seniors

For Graduating Seniors: After you show me credible written proof from the Registrar that you are graduating this CURRENT semester (e.g., spring graduation does not count for fall semester students), you may opt out of taking the final exam, using the following formula for calculating your final grade: Midterm would be worth 70%/Individual Project 30%

You may choose to take the final exam. If so, I will calculate the highest average for you: either the standard percentages listed in the syllabus or the above opt out formula. This, you "cannot lose" by sitting for the final exam.

If you wish to be considered for either option, you need to notify me in person on the date referenced in the syllabus.

APPENDIX M
Faculty Praise for the Author's Last Book, *Classroom LIGHTBULBS for College Professors* (2023)

Recognition & Awards

#1 Amazon New Release in Pedagogy (January 2023)
2023 Gold Medal E-Lit Book Award in Education/Academic/Teaching
2023 Finalist Readers Favorite Book Award in Non-Fiction/Education

Education Media

"Much good advice from a very enthusiastic and imaginative teacher."
Jay Mathews, *Washington Post* education columnist

College

"*Classroom LIGHTBULBS* is inspirational in its depiction of the author's irrepressible enthusiasm for teaching and his deep feeling for his students in and out of the classroom."
Elizabeth T. Tricomi, Ph.D., Director of ESL Program and the Writing Center (Retired), Binghamton University

"I recommend Professor Binder's book to anyone who wants a unique and motivational perspective when it comes to teaching. It is for both new and seasoned instructors and provides many illuminating examples filled with grit, pathos, and humor."
David Orozco, J.D., Bank of America Professor of Business Administration, Florida State University

"*Classroom LIGHTBULBS* is an invaluable resource for teachers in all disciplines to make learning infectious in the post-pandemic era! Binder is engaging, humorous, and charismatic as he demonstrates how to masterfully engage students. I have successfully implemented a number of his strategies in my biology courses, and I look forward to further adapting his 'lightbulbs' in all my classes."
Paul Ulrich, Ph.D., Principal Senior Lecturer, Department of Biology, Georgia State University

"In *Classroom LIGHTBULBS,* Perry Binder shares how he forms connections with students from their first interaction, throughout the semester, and beyond. He teaches the importance of learning to recognize that students come from all different backgrounds and experiences; thus, helping educators foster an engaging learning in law and academia, along with his creative use of humor and engagement, inspires a love of learning which leaves lasting impressions beyond the classroom."

Collyn W. Alford, M.S., Higher Ed. Admission & Advising Professional/Recruitment Outreach Specialist, University of Virginia School of Continuing & Professional Studies

"The Lightbulb certainly went on many times over, as I read *Classroom LIGHTBULBS*. Dr. Binder has certainly relayed exciting and practical activities to engage students, to build those crucial professor/student relationships, and to get students thinking in creative and divergent ways. This book reflects theory through practice by utilizing engaging stories of his passionate classroom experiences. I found myself thinking of the benefits of this book for new professors and for any educator willing to try new approaches. This is a winner!"

Deb L. Marciano, Ph.D., Teacher Educator (Retired), Valdosta State University

High School

"As educators, it is our passion to not only teach our content area, but to guide and mentor, support and love, and entertain and bring smiles. *Classroom LIGHTBULBS* is full of wonderful examples of how to do just that."

Ryan Yard, Ed.S., Georgia Teacher

"Professor Binder has written the perfect beginners manual for the new instructor. As a high school teacher, I recognize in Professor Binder's writing the kind of attention to detail required to reach students. He delivers the needed steps in this book for teachers to administer student centered learning which leads to discovery. I have known Professor Binder since middle school. He is my longtime friend and he was my teacher, even then. His *LIGHTBULBS* has been in development even then as he helped me to pass high school chemistry using the same principles he espoused in his book. This book is the model of sincerity. It comes from the heart."

Paul Cohen, M.A., NYC Science Teacher and Coordinator of Forensic & Earth Sciences

APPENDIX N
Classroom LIGHTBULBS Acronym

The LIGHTBULBS acronym illustrates a technique I use to stay motivated and focused on classroom excellence:

Listen to all learners
Inspire students with real world discussions
Give hope to everyone
Help students stay engaged through exaggeration and humor
Teach to your strengths

Be available at all times, whether in person or electronically
Understand that students may lack your life experience or knowledge
Let your passion rub off on students
Be willing to walk in your students' shoes
Stay within yourself?

The acronym highlights ten universal qualities of Master Teachers. Each letter of the LIGHTBULBS is supported with my unique teaching perspectives on student engagement, compassion, and justice, as told through humorous, serious, and relatable stories from the classroom and life experiences. These anecdotes serve as an easy way for me to remember to apply the acronym and get fired up to teach before walking into class. Later in the book, I provide "Binder's Reminders for Classroom Motivation"—short prompts to a story from its corresponding LIGHTBULBS chapter.

The Reminders are intended to have you think about your most memorable adventures from the classroom and beyond. Jot them down and use this in the future to apply the acronym. On days when you feel unmotivated to teach, re-read these notes as a reminder of the value you bring into the classroom and your students' lives. Do this a few times as a way to get fired up for an upcoming class.

Finally, the LIGHTBULBS method was not formulated in a light bulb moment. While my subject matter area is business law, this book should resonate with all disciplines. As you read each chapter, continually think about how it translates in a meaningful way to your discipline and teaching approach.

APPENDIX O
Author's Publications

Teacher Guide

Justice Cases for the Classroom: Teacher Guide on Legal Underdog Lessons (2017)

Books

Classroom Lightbulbs for College Professors (2023)

99 *Motivators for College Success* (2012)

Unlocking Your Rubber Room—44 Off-the-Wall Lessons to Lighten and Transform Everyday Life (2009)

Select Articles

Articles written for the College Section of *The Huffington Post* on teaching justice issues, college/career tips, and humor in the classroom:

"Achieving Justice: Legal Underdogs & Outcomes of Yes, No & Maybe," Apr. 2, 2017

"Jesse Friedman's Case and the Appearance of Impropriety," January 8, 2015

"Is Actual Innocence 'Capturing the Friedmans,' 25 Years Later?," November 27, 2012

"10 Tips for Picking a Career Path in College," August 7, 2012

"10 Tips for Thriving in College Life," August 3, 2012

"10 Classroom Tips for Your First College Semester," July 31, 2012

"7 Things the Amanda Knox Case Taught Us about Studying Abroad," October 9, 2011

"The Upcoming 9/11 Trial isn't about Money but Elusive Justice," August 11, 2011

"Lessons of Justice for College Students: Grandpa versus Big Coal," October 27, 2010

" 'Capturing the Friedmans' Dad Was My Unforgettable Teacher: Apply His Classroom Lessons to Set His Son Free," August 25, 2010

"The Case for Humor in the College Classroom," August 13, 2010 (first published in the AJC)

Academic Journal Articles/Business Cases

Work in Progress: Perry Binder, "Non-Competes and Workplace Morale—A Class Exercise"

Perry Binder, "Teaching Consumer Law & Advocacy Skills with a Judge Judy Team Project," 31 *Midwest Law Journal* 27–60 (2021)

Perry Binder, Susan L. Willey & Harold Weston, "Teaching Workplace Privacy Issues with a Big Data Group Project," 37(2) *Journal of Legal Studies Education* 185–244 (2020)

Perry Binder, "The Entrepreneurs with No Garage Project: Protecting Ownership Interests and Intellectual Property on a Shoestring Budget," 2(2) *Journal of Business Law and Ethics Pedagogy* 6–28 (2019)

Perry Binder, "Firing Employees for Their Social Media Posts: Ethical and Legal Issues," *Sage Business Cases* (2019)

Perry Binder, "Creating Social Media Law Projects to Sensitize Business Students to Appropriate Digital Conduct," 27 *Southern Law Journal* 327–366 (2017)

Perry Binder, "Flipping a Law Class Session: Creating Effective Online Content and Real World In-Class Team Modules," 17 *Atlantic Law Journal* 34–69 (2015)

Perry Binder and Nancy R. Mansfield, "Social Networks and Workplace Risk: Classroom Scenarios from a U.S. and EU Perspective," 30 *Journal of Legal Studies Education* 1–44 (2013)

Perry Binder, "New Top-Level Domain Names Add .Xxxtra Company Burden—Group Scenarios to Create Effective Domain Registration Portfolios," 14 *Atlantic Law Journal* 114–145 (2012)

Practitioner Chapters

American Jurisprudence, Proof of Facts

Perry Binder, "Liability for Airing False or Misleading Television Infomercials," 37 AM JUR POF 3D, 259–314 (1996)

Perry Binder, "Sports Memorabilia Dealer's Liability to Collector," 33 AM JUR POF 3D 359–420 (1995)

Perry Binder, "Proof of Music Sampling in Copyright Infringement," 26 AM JUR POF 3D 537–628 (1994)

Perry Binder, "Liability of Private Trade School to Student," 22 AM JUR POF 3D 411–484 (1993)

Perry Binder, "Copyright Infringement of a Screenplay," 18 AM JUR POF 3D 721–804 (1992)

Acknowledgments

In my last book, I thanked every colleague, editor, and friend under the sun. This prompted a professor to email me about his own recent book: "I don't think I got past 18–20 names last time." Well, I might've thanked four times that total. Let me thank them all again here and rather than repeat everyone's name, take this time to highlight and thank the Master Teachers in *Innovative College Teaching* from the bottom of my heart. Each of you helped make this a special year for me: Diana S. Barber, Jordan (Jody) Blanke, Yelena Abalmazova Chan, Evaristo Fernando Doria, L. Gregory (Greg) Henley, Leila Lawlor, Laura E. Meyers, Isabelle N. Monlouis, Benita Harris Moore, Carol Springer Sargent, John P. Thielman, Paul Ulrich, and Marta Szabo White.

About the Author

Perry Binder, J.D. is an award-winning author and professor, who has taught full-time at research-1 and technical colleges, and part-time at community colleges. Presently, Perry teaches graduate and undergraduate law classes at Georgia State University's Robinson College of Business. His book, *Classroom LIGHTBULBS for College Professors*, debuted as a #1 Amazon New Release in Pedagogy (January 2023) and received the 2023 Gold Medal e-Lit Award in Education/Academic/Teaching. Each year from 2016–2022, Perry's book, *99 Motivators for College Success*, was sent to hundreds of rising high school seniors nationwide, as part of the Book Award Program at Randolph College in Virginia.

For More Information

InnovativeCollegeTeaching.com

Social Media

Instagram @Perry_Binder
X (Twitter) @Perry_Binder
YouTube @Perry_Binder

Made in United States
Orlando, FL
08 January 2024